understand your kids and enjoy parenting

A PRACTICAL GUIDE TO CHILD PSYCHOLOGY

KAIREN CULLEN

C334193847

This edition published in the UK
in 2018 by Icon Books Ltd,
Omnibus Business Centre,
39–41 North Road,
London N7 9DP
email: info@iconbooks.com
www.iconbooks.com

First published in the UK
in 2011 by Icon Books

Sold in the UK, Europe and Asia
by Faber & Faber Ltd,
Bloomsbury House,
74–77 Great Russell Street,
London WC1B 3DA
or their agents

Distributed in South Africa
by Jonathan Ball,
Office B4, The District,
41 Sir Lowry Road,
Woodstock 7925

Distributed in Australia and
New Zealand
by Allen & Unwin Pty Ltd,
PO Box 8500,
83 Alexander Street,
Crows Nest,
NSW 2065

Distributed in Canada
by Publishers Group Canada,
76 Stafford Street, Unit 300
Toronto,
Ontario M6J 2S1

Distributed in the USA
by Publishers Group West,
1700 Fourth Street,
Berkeley, CA 94710

ISBN: 978-178578-322-7

Text copyright © 2011 Kairen Cullen

Typeset in Avenir by Marie Doherty

Printed and bound in the UK by Clays Ltd, St Ives plc

About the author

Dr Kairen Cullen is a chartered psychologist who trained as an educational psychologist and achieved a PhD at the Institute of Education, University of London. She has worked independently and in Local Education Authority contexts for over 38 years and has provided applied psychology services to schools and the community in a range of fields including education, health, sport and the media. She was chair of the Division of Educational and Child Psychology, British Psychological Society (BPS) in 2002 and continues to contribute actively to the work of the Society through media and consultation work. She has written for a number of academic and educational publications including the *Times Educational Supplement* and *5 to 7* and *Childcare* magazines. She regularly accepts writing and media work commissions and most recently has worked as the on-screen psychologist for an ITV series on parents and children and also contributed to celebrity best-seller Katie Piper's book *From Mother to Daughter* (Quercus, 2018).

Author's note

It's important to note that there is much frequently-used research employed in child psychology. Where I know the source I have been sure to reference it, but my apologies here to the originators of any material if I have overlooked them.

Contents

INTRODUCTION

1. The reasons behind this book

Everyone needs to understand children better, and so most people will find the ideas in this book useful.

> *A policy which gives priority to investment in children would give practical recognition to the fact that they are the seed-corn of the future. Their development determines the fabric of tomorrow's society.*
> Mia Kellmer-Pringle

You may be wondering: 'Will this book help me to "psychologize" my child?'

The answer is a definite no. We live in very psychological times. Turn on the television, the internet, the radio, or open a magazine or newspaper, and I guarantee you will read, see or hear something of a psychological nature very quickly. Most people use some amateur psychology, but this is very different to the work of a professional psychologist who, along with many years of study and supervised professional practice, must always try to work with objectivity, neutrality and scientific rigour. Actually, there are many areas of psychological theory that use the idea that we are all psychologists in our own lives, and I will be explaining more about that later.

In the following pages there are many activities and exercises to help you get a firm grasp of the ideas presented. Some of them may be fun and safe to try out with your own children, and if this is the case the book will make this clear. One of the major complications of studying and researching children is that it's not acceptable to do anything that could in any way harm the child's well-being, and so it's always important to err on the side of caution. For this reason, many of the activities must be done with an imaginary child. It might help to start reading this book with your imaginary child in mind, and perhaps the one you can create most easily will be the one that was once you!

This book will offer some ideas that will help you to understand children better. People are complex and children are perhaps even more so, as they by definition are learning, developing and changing constantly and rapidly. Add to this the fact that each child's situation and history is unique, and it's obvious that the better equipped you are to understand, the more likely you are to be able to contribute something useful and to help support the child's learning and development. Fortunately – or maybe unfortunately, depending on your perspective – there's no recipe book or manual for helping a child become a healthy, functional and happy adult person, but there are many well-theorized and well-researched ideas that psychology can offer in doing the best job possible – and most are ones you will recognize from everyday life, as the renowned paediatrician Benjamin

Spock acknowledges in his book on child development and parenting: 'You know more than you think you do.'

One word of caution, though: there are certain problematic issues that can arise in a child's learning, development and/or behaviour, which require the input of appropriately qualified professionals. If the child's overall development, well-being and/or health is significantly different to that of the majority of other children in their age group, and is causing concern, it's important to seek advice. The family doctor and/or the child's teacher are generally good starting points for getting this help. Even the best-equipped and most knowledgeable parents and carers need professional support at times.

I think that, as for most aspects of the complex human world, supporting the development, learning and behaviour of children is best viewed as a continuous, everyday problem-solving or solution-producing process. To take part in this process with vitality and realistic optimism requires considerable energy and stamina, to say nothing of confidence. When I was a parent of four young children I would have liked to have heard this perspective rather than the usual 'this is the approach/method/package that will answer all of your questions and solve any problems regardless of your situation, resources or history'. I am hoping that this small book on child psychology will offer something different: some fresh, accessible and useful ideas that readers can draw upon in their involvement with their unique children.

2. What is a child?

The main aim of child psychology is to help us know how best to raise and care for our children. This is an ambitious aim, as so many factors and processes have to be taken into account and there is so much individual variation in the rate at which children develop and mature. The logical starting point is to define what is meant by the term 'child'. Try this for yourself and just jot down your definition of a child. Ask others you meet today the same question. By the end of the day you will probably have noted quite a few different points. Some of these may reflect the view that a child is simply a miniature adult, a prevalent view until relatively recent times. Others may relate to children's early stage in human development, highlighting the things a child cannot do. Then you may have other viewpoints that children have some special, albeit temporary gifts and strengths, quite distinct from those of adults.

Can we simply use the legal definition, i.e. number of years lived? If it's merely a matter of being below or above the age of majority, then that's relatively straightforward and definitions of the term 'child' should be consistent across time and also different parts of the world. However, we know, at a common sense level, that this is an inadequate definition that doesn't take into account the wide variety of levels of maturity, independence and responsibility that some under-18-year-olds exhibit. Is it to do with the child's ability, skills and knowledge, or maybe their level of understanding? Erik Erikson, a famous psychologist who has developed a theory of understanding human development over the entire life-span and whose work we will look at specifically in a later chapter, reminds us of the added complication of sexual maturity:

> *With the establishment of a good relationship to the world of skills and tools, and with the advent of sexual maturity, childhood proper comes to an end.*
> Erik Erikson, *Childhood and Society*, 1950

Perhaps the key to defining childhood lies in the child's role and place in the family and their degree of dependency on older family members? In the developed western world it's relatively uncommon for under-18s to be supporting families through paid employment or to be caring for very young children or unwell and/or elderly relatives. In fact, it's actually the case that financial dependency on parents carries on long past the late teens for an increasing number of families. This is not reflected in all parts of the world, though, and child psychology recognizes that social, cultural and environmental influences play a major part in the way in which we define a child and the way in which theory is developed and research on children is undertaken.

What do you think of this idea?

> *The proper time to influence the character of a child is about a hundred years before he is born.*
> W.R. Inge, *The Observer*, 21 July 1929

Do you agree that historical and social factors are responsible for the way a child behaves, feels and thinks?

And what about this idea:

> *Nothing has a stronger influence psychologically on their environment, and especially on their children, than the unlived life of their parents.*
> Carl Jung (1875–1961), *Paracelsus*

Are the hopes, wishes and expectations of the parents such a major factor in the child's development, in your experience?

The quiz that follows has been designed to show the importance of the ideas you hold about childhood in your parenting and work with children. Research across the world has identified some very different child-rearing practices of mothers with infants. These are listed in column 1. Try to match each example with the countries listed in column 2.

Child-rearing practices	Country
1. Teaching rather than play, as play is seen as unnecessary and inappropriate.	**A**. India
2. Constant skin-to-skin contact between mothers and infants, including sleeping together.	**B**. New Zealand – Maori
3. Largely facial and verbal communication with child rather than hand displays.	**C**. Japan
4. Daily massage of infants.	**D**. America
5. Limited tickling and lap-bouncing.	**E**. Kenya
6. Little face-to-face interaction between mother and infant.	**F**. Mexico
7. The mother's main aim is to achieve a calm and easily cared-for child, and so all emotional arousal is discouraged.	**G**. New Guinea

1 – F In research with low-income Mexican mothers, the emphasis on work, i.e. the serious nature of life and the frivolous nature of play, was apparent in the mothers' focus on useful instruction rather than play with their babies.

2 – C Japanese babies are viewed as being separate, essentially unconnected beings at birth and the mother's primary role is to socialize and create strong interpersonal connections between herself and the baby. The commonly perceived Japanese tendency to conformism and group membership is seen by some as another aspect of this view.

3 – D In this example the social communication style of adult Americans is highlighted in the way in which mothers communicate with their infants.

4 – B The effect of cultural traditions of a baby's birthplace on the child's development is demonstrated in the Maori daily ritual of massage.

5 – A Indian parents tend to engage in games such as 'Peek-a-Boo!' rather than whole-body games. This may reflect different aims within early child-rearing practices, i.e. greater emphasis on cognitive development (perception, thinking and learning) than on physical development.

6 – G The babies of New Guinea mothers are encouraged from the start to face away from their mothers and to interact with others. This is necessary as New Guinea families tend to live communally and the mother–child unit is viewed as secondary to the group membership.

7 – E Kenyan mothers must return to their work in the fields as quickly as possible after the birth of their babies, and so the priority is to raise affable, placid babies, whom others can easily care for in the mother's absence.

An awareness of the many different views of what is normal for children and for parents and the influence of different cultures and living situations is important. It also contributes to an understanding of the nature/nurture debate: which factors and qualities are innate to the child, or genetic, and which come from their experience of the places and situations into which they are born and live? As you will discover, much child psychology theory and research has contributed to this debate, and neither side looks likely to win! Child psychology reflects a nature *and* nurture standpoint rather than nature *or* nurture, and it has influenced many government-funded national projects to support children's development and well-being, for example the American 'Headstart' and the UK's 'Sure Start' pre-school enrichment programmes.

3. What is psychology?

*Psychology: the science that tells you what you already
know in words you don't understand and gives you ideas
you wish you could have thought of on your own.*

Anon.

Psychology is all about understanding and studying human
minds and behaviour, and child psychology focuses on children and their development.

Many theories and associated approaches and methods for the study of psychology have developed and continue to evolve, and it's not unusual for a new theory to be
proclaimed as the best and only theory worth using. History
teaches us to be wary, for in the course of psychology's
relatively short existence, a number of claims of this type
have been made for major psychological theories. These
'grand theories', as they are known, include behaviourism,
psychoanalytical, humanist and cognitive approaches, and
they can usually be detected in the theoretical frameworks
available today. It would be true to say that each time a theoretical framework rises in popularity, another one develops and may be viewed as a more useful and appropriate
framework for its time.

In this wide and complex field of enquiry no single
theory or approach can claim to have all the answers. Every
theory, by definition, generates better understanding and

insight and subsequently more complex theory. George Kelly, to whom a chapter is devoted later in the book, brought a blend of psychoanalytical and cognitivist theory together, to create his Personal Construct Theory. The following quote sums up a useful and useable approach to the question of 'What is theory?'

A theory may be considered a way of binding together a multitude of facts so that one may comprehend them all at once. When the theory enables us to make reasonably precise predictions, one may call it scientific ... our anticipations of daily events, whilst not scientifically precise nevertheless surround our lives with an aura of meaning. A theory provides a basis for an active approach to life, not merely a comfortable armchair to contemplate its vicissitudes with detached complaisance.

George Kelly

It's doubtful that many parents take the 'armchair' approach to parenting in a literal sense. Children generally make this impossible! In terms of developing their own unique theories of parenting – and I genuinely believe this is what all parents do, albeit mainly at an unconscious level – the majority of parents are active and creative. This book will hopefully contribute more material for this everyday theory-making. At this point it will be helpful to consider some aspects of each of the major theoretical approaches and see how these ideas might look in reality.

Behaviourist

View of human beings	Research methods	Criticisms
1. All human behaviour is learnt through experience in the real world, i.e. through trying things out; and if the result is rewarding, doing more of it, and if not, doing less of it.	1. Only observable and measurable behaviours are investigated.	1. Seen as reducing humans to physical organisms with no 'inner' emotional and/or mental aspects.
2. Learning in animals and humans happens in the same way, i.e. as explained in 1. above.	2. Findings from animal experimentation are seen as being directly relevant to humans.	2. Humans and animals cannot be compared or seen as sharing the same drives and behaviours.
3. Mental or emotional aspects viewed as unimportant in determining the person's actions.	3. Mental or emotional processes, which cannot be measured or controlled, cannot be part of scientific enquiry.	3. Just because you can't measure an aspect of human behaviour, this doesn't justify dismissing its usefulness.

Pure behaviourist theory is based on the idea that humans do more of a certain type of behaviour if they get rewarded for it, or less if they are punished in some way, just like a pigeon pecking a lever harder and more often when it releases a seed, or a child not touching a hot radiator when s/he gets burnt from doing so.

CASE STUDY

Think of your imaginary child and imagine if the very first time they met a dog, it was a particularly large and angry specimen that barked and growled ferociously at them. In behaviourist theory, this child's experience has resulted in them learning that dogs are aggressive and frightening and make them feel unsafe. If the child has no further, more positive contact with dogs, or has other, similarly threatening experiences, it's possible that an extreme anxiety condition or even a phobia of dogs could result. A psychologist using a purely behavioural approach would attempt to reduce the child's associations between dogs and these difficult feelings by 'exposing' them, in a gradual and controlled manner, to other dogs that are friendly and not threatening and enabling them to actually have enjoyable, happy experiences. This way the child would have new information that can balance out and reduce the previous negative experience. They can then learn that only some dogs that behave in certain ways are to be feared, and can shape their own behaviour accordingly.

Psychoanalytical

View of human beings	Research methods	Criticisms
1. Human behaviour is mainly controlled by subconscious associations and inner processes.	1. Undertaken as individual therapy over time.	1. Lacking in rigour and structure that can be replicated by other researchers.
2. The early life of the infant is the time when these associations and processes develop.	2. Emphasis on processes rather than measurable and easily described behaviour.	2. Analyst is viewed as lacking in necessary objectivity.
3. People develop psychological defences in order to deal with problematic situations, events and relationships.	3. Main goal of psychoanalytical enquiry is to bring together the individual's inner life and behaviour in order to achieve well-being.	3. Psychoanalysis takes a long time and is costly.

REMEMBER THIS!!! Psychoanalytical theory recommends that people should spend many hours, often on a couch, telling their therapist about their earliest memories, dreams and deepest fears, so that they can feel better now.

CASE STUDY **Think of your imaginary child** and imagine that they have woken in a distressed state, having had a bad dream about being bitten by a wild bear. A purely psychoanalytical approach would involve talking for a long time with the child, if they were old enough, over many sessions, and encouraging them to express their feelings and to make connections with situations and experiences in their real life (as opposed to their imaginary dream life). The 'treatment' might also use play and drawing activities to aid the process.

Humanist

View of human beings	Research methods	Criticisms
1. Human behaviour is largely driven by the need to belong, to achieve, and to have some control.	1. The emphasis is on people's perspectives and the sense that they make of their experience in the world.	1. Does not take the real world into account, e.g. financial and political aspects.
2. Sees humans as complex and unique individuals.	2. The researcher as a person is viewed as a part of any enquiry, and their perspective and beliefs need to be accounted for.	2. Lack of objectivity and need for practical application.
3. The meaning-making of people is seen as more important than objective, observable behaviour.	3. Each person's view of the world is unique, and no comparison with others, or value judgement, is placed.	3. Most extreme behaviours and mental health problems are hard to understand in this approach.

In humanist theory, the researcher is the audience for each person's special production of 'This is how I see the world' and should listen, watch and applaud.

Think of your imaginary child and imagine that they are experiencing problems with other children at school, feeling left out and unpopular. The psychologist using a purely humanist approach would try to find lots of affirming activities and talk to give the child more positive self-esteem. They would listen very carefully and attempt to understand in a non-judgemental way the child's story. They might share their own experiences in a relevant way if they considered this could be helpful. They would work to equip the child with skills and expectations that supported friendship with other children.

Cognitive

View of human beings	Research methods	Criticisms
1. Human behaviour can be made sense of in information-processing terms, i.e. in a similar way to a computer.	1. Cognitive research aims to understand the rules by which people act.	1. The amount of information to be taken into account is potentially enormous.
2. People act with purpose according to the information they have.	2. The researcher suggests a complex set of rules or ideas, known as a schema, and tests their ideas out by collecting evidence that shows whether the schema is accurate or not.	2. Much of the research must be done on the basis of guesswork and prediction.
3. Learning happens as feedback is received from the behaviour choices that a person makes.	3. All research is carried out in the belief that human behaviour is logical and structured according to rules.	3. Research can generally focus only on information available in the here and now.

Cognitive theory is concerned with perception, thinking, learning and problem-solving. It views human behaviour like a complex computer, and research is designed to crack the code and system by which the computer works.

Think of your imaginary child and imagine that they are experiencing difficulties with learning about number. A psychologist using a purely cognitive approach would focus on the information-processing aspects of their learning, i.e. the information available to them about number, their understanding of the concept of number, the rules for application of this concept, their storage and processing capacities, and their recall and use of this understanding and learning. They would consider the child's age and developmental level in relation to how such information was presented, and the types of information and ways of using it that were made available. For example, children of nursery age generally need lots of concrete, hands-on information about number such as counting activities with actual objects. The psychologist would work with the child and with the adults responsible for supporting the child's learning, such as parents, carers and nursery staff.

*

The aim of this book is to present a broad view of the psychological theories that contribute to our understanding of child psychology. The book is organized into four main sections, corresponding with the four major approaches just described. I have tried to select each major theory and fit it into one of the sections, but I must stress that there's a great deal of overlap because so many ideas owe their origins and/or development to either behaviourist, psychoanalytical, humanist or cognitive psychology. Inevitably some theories that are used in child psychology practice just cannot be fitted into these four main categories, so I have added an additional theories section, which includes some information about social psychology and ecological systems theories.

REMEMBER THIS!!!

1. Psychology is the scientific study of human behaviour and experience.
2. Psychological research is undertaken in order to build on existing research and theory in order to create even better theories and research.
3. Research is generally undertaken by focusing on the rich detail of individual experience and behaviour or on large groups of people, from which generalizations may be drawn.
4. Four main theoretical frameworks have developed: behaviourist, psychoanalytical, cognitive and humanist.

4. Applied psychology practice

If there are so many theories, and no one theory has all the answers or covers everything, why do we need theories at all? A theory is generally a collection of scientifically tried and tested ideas that have been investigated in a structured and rigorous manner. When it comes to spending large amounts of money in trying to make people's lives safer, more rewarding and healthier, theory is generally a better basis than uninformed opinion for knowing what resources, actions and methods are needed. Look at the following situations and decide for yourself whether you would rather seek advice from a friend or relative who had been through a similar situation, or from a qualified professional:

- Your child stops wanting to play with friends.
- Your son's school has told you that they think he has specific learning difficulties and is struggling to learn how to read and write.
- Your daughter says she doesn't want to go to school each morning and becomes very distressed, but won't explain why.
- You think your son is stealing.

You may have hesitated and even decided that another parent or a relative would have been your preferred first stop for talking through your worries, but the difficulty with everyday problem-solving is that it's generally based on ideas that come from and work well in one individual's day-to-day life. This means that their own weak spots or hobby horses can influence the advice they give, and can even do harm. In the case of a professional, they will be systematically drawing on years of study, familiarity with up-to-date research and theory, and, very importantly, on a code of professional practice and ethics. The box below summarizes one such code, and I think it would be fair to say that advice from a friend or relative is unlikely to offer this range of safeguards.

The British Psychological Society's Code of Ethics and Conduct	
The four main principles and what they should mean in practice for any person using chartered psychologist services	
RESPECT	The client should be treated with dignity and sensitivity, and should experience privacy, choice and a sense of worth.
COMPETENCE	The psychologist should offer high levels of relevant and up-to-date knowledge, skill, training, education, and experience.
INTEGRITY	Psychologists should work with honesty, accuracy, transparency and fairness in all their dealings as professionals and scientists.
RESPONSIBILITY	Psychologists should be aware of their responsibility to bring benefit to the client, to the public, to society and to science, and also to do no harm or to risk their expertise being misused.

Many different types of applied psychology have developed since psychology became a discipline in its own right. These include: counselling psychology, clinical psychology, educational psychology, occupational psychology, sports and exercise psychology, health psychology, occupational psychology and neuropsychology, and all have their own systems of training.

It's possible for applied psychologists to work with children and young people from all of these divisions, but it's fair to say that most practitioners who use the title 'child psychologist' are from either clinical or educational psychology backgrounds. The important thing to remember, if you ever wish to use the services of someone calling themselves a child psychologist, is that they are chartered and listed on the British Psychological Society Register of Child Psychologists (details are listed in the reference section, along with relevant details for other countries).

In my work as an educational psychologist, every issue or problem that is presented becomes the basis for research in order to find out as much accurate, relevant information as possible from as wide a field as possible. The aim is always to gain some better understanding so that useful ideas for addressing the issue can be suggested, and then hopefully put into action. Every piece of work is unique, and it could involve an individual child or adult, a group, a class, a school year group, or maybe even a whole school. Going back to the question of theory: real-life issues rarely fit neatly into one theoretical approach, so it's important to have a grasp of as much theory as possible. This means lots of reading and learning in order to be as well informed as possible and to have a wide range of ideas to draw upon. This book doesn't claim to be definitive or comprehensive in terms of the huge topic of child psychology, but it does offer an exploration of some of the most important theories, some interesting research findings, examples from the work of child psychologists, and some discussion about their contributions to child psychology.

COGNITIVE THEORY

5. Piaget

I noticed with amazement that the simplest reasoning task ... presented, for normal children up to the age of eleven or twelve, difficulties unsuspected by the adult.

Jean Piaget (1896–1980)

Ironically, the first big theory we're going to look at was developed by an academic who initially wasn't a psychologist at all. But despite this, Jean Piaget is credited with being the second most cited psychologist ever, after Freud. He was also the most criticized, but in psychology this isn't necessarily viewed as such a bad thing, because his ideas stimulated so much further research and theory.

Piaget became a major figure in developmental psychology and created some important ideas from his early biological research, initially with molluscs and other animals, that have contributed a lot to our understanding of children's development and learning. He was born in the late 19th century in Switzerland and became fascinated by the way children learn. He asked some big questions about whether they came pre-set, with certain fixed individual capacities to learn, or whether the kind of learning opportunities they were given could increase their cognitive development. Piaget was interested in the **process** of learning rather than simply describing the content of it, and he based his theory on many hours of direct observation of children in different learning situations. Thinking back to the previous chapter and the four major theoretical frameworks – behaviourist, psychoanalytical, humanist and cognitive – you will see that Piaget's developmental ideas arise from a **cognitive model** of human development.

Cognitive – comes from the Latin meaning 'to learn' or 'to know' and refers to processes and activities involved in perception, thinking, learning and problem-solving.

Piaget used many observations of his own children to build his theory, and one well known example is as follows.

Piaget noticed that when one of his daughters, Jacqueline, aged seven months, dropped her plastic duck beneath the fold of a blanket, and therefore out of sight, she appeared to lose all interest straight away in retrieving the toy she had been enjoying so much. Piaget then picked up the duck, presented it to his daughter and, clearly in her view, placed it back beneath the blanket. Again, she made no effort to get it back. He tried this over and over again and got the same reaction. It was as though, because the little girl couldn't see the duck, it had ceased to exist for her, i.e. out of sight, out of mind. Piaget tried this activity with other very young children, and as he invariably got the same kind of response he deduced that until at least nine or ten months of age, children just hadn't had enough experience of the world to appreciate **object permanence** – to know that objects continued to exist, whether or not they could be directly experienced.

Try putting a play object out of sight from a child of less than eight or nine months and you're likely to see a similar reaction to Piaget's Jacqueline. Do you think this seeming lack of interest might be to do with the child's memory capacity? Maybe they're just not mature enough to select and hold on to information about something that's not in their direct view? Perhaps their visual–motor coordination hasn't developed to the stage where they can actually reach for something not in their line of vision?

Another reason for the child's seeming inability to appreciate object permanence might be that a very young child is so reliant on, and tuned into, their parent's behaviour that if the parent behaves as though an object no longer exists, then the child takes the parental cue and doesn't waste energy behaving any differently.

In fact, many studies of small children carried out since Piaget's initial work have actually found that children as young as three and a half months can understand that an object continues to exist even though they can't see it.

Another famous study that Piaget carried out was his 'mountain experiment'. In this, a seven-year-old child is presented with a toy landscape with roads, houses, mountains, etc., and also a doll that is placed in such a way as to be viewing the landscape in a different direction to the child. The child is then asked to describe what they think the doll can see. The child and even older children of eight or more usually describe the scene that they can see. Piaget called this an inability to **de-centre** – that is, to see from another's perspective – and the only way they can develop a more mature, accurate and less egocentric perspective is to have many concrete and social learning experiences. This has very important implications for schools, suggesting that children need lots of active and 'enquiry-based' learning. Early years and primary education have been especially influenced by Piaget's discoveries.

Tell me and I'll forget; show me and I may remember; involve me and I'll understand.
Chinese proverb

Another of Piaget's big ideas is illustrated in an experiment in which he presents a child with different-sized, see-through containers, into which he pours liquid. Each container is filled with exactly the same amount of liquid but because some are taller and slimmer or shorter and wider, children at a pre-operational level (two to seven years; see table on p. 33) find it difficult to appreciate this fact. They will guess that the amount of liquid increases the taller the container, and vice versa for shorter but wider containers. The operational-level child (seven to eleven), however, can increasingly use logic and deduction and when presented with this task is able to conserve their knowledge of the effects of container size and volume and will realize that the amount of liquid stays the same, despite its surface level rising.

 You can easily and safely try this experiment with your own child. Fill a measuring jug with their favourite drink at a time when they're ready for some liquid refreshment. Then line up several transparent cups of different heights and widths, and pour the same amount of drink into each. Then call your child into the room and ask them to choose one. By the way, if there's a favourite cup, don't use this one, as it would 'skew' or distort the experiment because your child would choose it regardless of how much drink they thought it contained. For a child in Piaget's pre-operational stage (approximately two to seven years), their judgement of which receptacle contains the most liquid will be poor. In other words, they won't understand how to judge a number of concepts such as space, volume, and dimension accurately and make logical deductions based on this.

Ideas about how children of different ages think and reason are important in understanding and supporting their learning. As Piaget said:

> It is with children that we have the best chance of studying the development of logical knowledge, mathematical knowledge, physical knowledge, and so forth.

Piaget's theory can help us to provide the best possible kinds of learning for children at different stages of cognitive development. From his early studies with molluscs, Piaget saw that just like the water snail, the child's learning and development happened as a result of the particular challenges of the environment in which s/he lived. Key ideas about learning and education have been drawn from Piaget's work, stressing the importance of having a genuine reason and purpose to learn, being actively involved, and providing lots of activity and enquiry-based learning opportunities. The idea of teaching children through individualized approaches in small groups rather than the traditional whole-class 'chalk and talk' approach comes largely from these ideas, and some educationalists such as Maria

Montessori created a whole early-years education system on the basis of them.

Teachers should try to provide lots of play-based learning in well-equipped, rich and stimulating environments for children in the sensori-motor stage (below two years of age). Children in the pre-operational and concrete operational stages (two to seven and seven to eleven respectively) need increasingly challenging learning activities that involve opportunities to classify, sort, order, locate and conserve using concrete objects. Children of eleven years and above need to be presented with complex and increasingly abstract and moral social issues and be allowed to reflect, research and discuss. Over time, the levels of adult support should decrease in order to help them to become increasingly independent and self-directing in their learning and problem-solving.

Piaget is famous for his **stage theory** of human cognitive development, and he saw this as the basis for other types of development such as social, emotional and moral. This theory maintains that every child goes through four age-related stages of cognitive development, which can be described in terms of the child's learning behaviour and also the major developmental challenges with which they need to grapple. Each stage builds on the previous one and cannot be skipped, a bit like climbing the rungs of a ladder. Have a look at the diagram that follows, which summarizes this.

Piaget's stage theory of cognitive development (how children acquire knowledge)

Sensori-motor: 0 to 2 years   • The child learns through senses and physical experience, e.g. shouting, banging, testing with their whole bodies.   • Key skills include learning that concrete objects stay the same, and also imitation.
Pre-operational: 2 to 7 years   • The child learns through increasing verbal and social interaction.   • Key skills include language development, symbolic concepts (e.g. number and letters), but they can't apply these ideas in a flexible way.   • Less egocentricity, i.e. more awareness of others.
Concrete operations : 7 to 11 years   • The child learns through structured educational experiences.   • Mastery of classes, relations, numbers.   • Logical reasoning, weight, measurement.
Formal operations (hypothetical reasoning): 11 years to adulthood   • The child engages in more and more sophisticated and abstract reasoning and thought.   • Broad social constructions such as justice and equality.

CASE STUDY

Piaget's idea that children learn what they need to learn according to the world they are born into is illustrated through the much-publicised 'feral children' studies. In these studies of children brought up by animals, thankfully very rare, the effects on their development were dramatically highlighted. Consider the various aspects of child development listed below. What animal do you think might have brought up the child displaying these features? (Answer below.)

Physical: Movement on all fours. Little fine motor movement and control, e.g. picking up small objects, using a spoon and other tools, early drawing.

Sensory: Sense of smell, taste, hearing, vision and touch highly developed for hunting and survival.

Cognitive: Little need for abstract reasoning, thinking, problem-solving of anything other than direct and immediate experience. Little imagination or creativity.

Language: Language would consist of grunts of different volume and would relate to primary needs and functions, which are of meaning in a pack.

Emotional: No language, so little expression or response to others, other than to extremes such as anger linked to aggression.

Social: Strong identification with the pack and little solitary or paired behaviour, friendship, or avoidance and constructive management of conflict.

Answer: wolf

Piaget's great and ambitious theory has many implications and has received a lot of attention over the decades, but subsequent research has revealed some shortcomings and inaccuracies in his ideas and the way in which the studies behind these ideas were conducted. Nevertheless, psychologists have much to thank him for, as a great deal of their research and work wouldn't have been possible without a grasp of the fundamental differences in the way children and adults think.

Four big ideas from Piaget

1. Children think very differently from adults, and understand the world according to their stage of cognitive development.
2. Cognitive development happens as a result of learning opportunities made available to the child – these opportunities must involve and engage the child so that they have to take in and use the ideas in their thinking, i.e. assimilation and accommodation.
3. It's important to provide the child with learning experiences that are not beyond their current stage of cognitive development.
4. The teacher must find a balance between engaging the child and also challenging them enough so they develop.

The last words in this chapter can be from Piaget, as he really did actively demonstrate the following principle upon which his work was based:

I think that human knowledge is essentially active.
Jean Piaget

6. Vygotsky

In general children do not create their own speech; they
master the existing speech of surrounding adults.
Lev Vygotsky (1896–1934)

Vygotsky and Piaget created their theories of development at about the same time, at the start of the 20th century. However, although both saw the environment of the growing child as key to the kind of learning that could happen, and the child as active in learning from the world, their ideas about the nature of this learning environment differed enormously. Piaget's idea that each child was equipped to learn particular things at particular ages didn't take into account the social and cultural aspects that were key to Vygotsky's theories. He emphasized the relationship between **thought** and **language**, presenting his theory that it's only through acquiring language and practical skills with the help of adults that the child's cognitive skills can mature.

Vygotsky's prolific career was curtailed at the age of 38 when he died of tuberculosis in 1934. Many of his ideas were disapproved of by the Soviet regime in which he lived, for he challenged popular notions of the time about human development. His major work *Thought and Language*, first published in 1934, was suppressed by the Soviet government until 1956. He rejected the theory that humans were born with fixed, biological capacities and simply learnt as a result of being 'fed' information from others. Instead, he highlighted the political and cultural influences with which the individual interacted throughout their development.

REMEMBER THIS!!!

A big idea from Vygotskian theory

The human social world is of major importance in the psychological development of individuals – and within this, language is central. This is often referred to as **Vygotsky's socio-cultural theory**. This theory is based on the idea that the history, location and culture of the person's birthplace is responsible for the kinds of learning they can experience and also for the cultural tools such as language, numeracy and technology that are available and that they can develop. These socio-cultural aspects are necessary for a shared understanding of the world and a similar way of thinking for members of the same society.

THINK ABOUT IT

We live in a world full of technology. Our children are exposed from a very young age to computers, mobile telephones, television and a host of other communication and entertainment facilities. What effects do you think this has on the development of:

Language – verbal, i.e. vocabulary, use of questions, social talk and non-verbal behaviour.

Cognitive skills – thinking, reasoning, problem-solving, computing, creativity and imagination.

Physical skills – fine motor skills, e.g. dexterity and use of small objects and tools such as drawing equipment, scissors, cutlery; and gross motor skills, e.g. running, jumping, climbing.

Social skills – friendship, leadership, conflict management skills. Being part of a group, understanding and following social rules, leadership.

Emotional skills – recognizing, managing, communicating and using emotions in self and others. Empathy, positive regard and being genuine.

Can you recall the less technologically developed world that you experienced as a young child? Think about the implications of these different learning experiences. Is it possible to be quite objective and analytical about this?

One of the terms for which Vygotsky is best known is the **Zone of Proximal Development** (ZPD). This refers to the idea that whenever learning takes place, the child starts from a position of existing knowledge and skill and reaches out to the limits of their ZPD to a new and unestablished learning position; and with the help, or in Vygotskian terms, mediation, of a more experienced and knowledgeable adult or other child, they move to this new position more easily. The diagram overleaf illustrates this idea.

1. Established skills and knowledge	2. Zone of Proximal Development	3. What the child can do with help. This gradually moves to a new position 1.

Zone of Proximal Development (ZPD)

Zone of Proximal Development (ZPD) – all possible learning and development that a child can achieve with effort, support and the right conditions.

At every stage of a child's development s/he will be on the verge of being able to understand and work out different learning problems. What s/he needs to crack the problem is structure, explanation, demonstration, prompts, tips and reminders, and lots of encouragement to boost confidence to keep trying. If s/he still can't solve the problem, then it's likely that it's just too difficult and is outside the child's ZPD. If, on the other hand, the child can solve the problem with help from an adult or a more knowledgeable child, then the problem lies within their ZPD.

An approach to the assessment of children's learning called **dynamic assessment** has developed from Vygotsky's work. This differs from more traditional assessment methods that measure a child's performance at the time of the assessment and then compare this to the average performance of children of a similar age. Dynamic assessment is less concerned with what the child has already learnt, or their current performance, than with what they are capable of learning – and specifically what is needed to help them achieve their full potential.

Remember the first time you used a telephone? You probably saw others using it, either directly in day-to-day life or vicariously, through viewed material such as film or television. This would have taught you about the purpose and function of a telephone, and this is the knowledge represented in box 1 in the ZPD diagram. The nitty gritty of *how* to use it required a more knowledgeable and experienced other to demonstrate and teach the skills of putting in a number, waiting for and responding to an answer, and carrying on a conversation. Box 2 in the ZPD diagram represents your readiness for this learning. Box 3 is where you would be after some help or mediation from an accomplished telephone-user. Once you had practised this new skill and used this new knowledge and gradually become more proficient in telephone use, you would then be in a new box 1 of established skills and knowledge and ready to extend the learning further through a new ZPD, for example using the telephone for making calls abroad.

Linked to Vygotsky's ZPD theory is the term **scaffolding**. This is what the more capable other person, an adult or child, offers to the child who is learning something new. This scaffolding is the support offered to the child in the form of encouragement, questions, a structured problem-solving approach, simplifying the task and allowing the child to do the simpler aspects to give them confidence, and instructions and demonstration. This process of scaffolding is more than just teaching or giving information. It's helping the child to develop some core problem-solving and thinking skills, which they can use and develop throughout their lives.

 Next time your child can't find an object, such as a toy or a piece of clothing, rather than just tell them where it is, ask some questions: 'Could it be in the garden?' 'Might it be in the kitchen?' 'Maybe it's in your bedroom?' Ask them to think of where they saw it last, or where they usually keep it. Ask if there might be someone else who knows where it could be. What you're doing here is mediating and offering scaffolding to give the child a firm base from which to solve the problem. You're also joining the child and collaborating in the problem-solving and offering lots of language, all of which is essential for learning. It's possible, too, that next time your child loses something, they will have learnt some skills that they can use on their own.

A word devoid of thought is a dead thing, and a thought unembodied in words remains a shadow.

Vygotsky

Vygotsky is responsible, above all, for making clear the links between thought and language at every stage of life, for everyone. His work on the role of private speech or talking to oneself demonstrates the fundamental difference between his and Piaget's ideas. Piaget saw this as an early and egocentric form of language, mainly used by the child to talk about themselves and their activities, but Vygotsky viewed it very differently. For him, this type of dialogue was an essential means of **cognitive processing**, frequently used by the young child for managing activities and giving instructions to themselves. He also noticed that as the child matured and became more sophisticated in learning and problem-solving, this kind of speech became internalized and gradually more and more unconscious. Interestingly, when learning or a problem-solving situation becomes more challenging, the talking-to-self strategy re-emerges. You can probably think of a situation where you've used this way of clarifying a problem and working out the solution.

Find a piece of very difficult reading material. It should be on a topic about which you know little. Read it first of all, silently. Now read it aloud. Now read it aloud and explain it, as you read, to someone else. Can you appreciate how breaking up the text, saying it aloud and also having to explain it, all help your learning? As the old saying goes: 'The best way to learn something is to teach it to somebody else.'

Key ideas from Vygotsky

- The child is an active participant in their learning and interaction with the world.
- The social and cultural aspects of a child's learning environment influence what kind of learning opportunities are available.
- Learning is a social process.
- The child's learning potential can be assessed by identifying the gap between solo and joint problem-solving, i.e. the child's ZPD.
- Teaching should be focused on the child's ZPD.
- The aim of effective teaching is to provide scaffolding and to gradually reduce this as the child becomes increasingly competent.

Vygotsky's work has led to a much greater understanding of children's learning and a great deal of further research that has supported important work in education. However, two main criticisms have been made. The first is that Vygotsky's work doesn't acknowledge the contribution of each child's **individuality** and places the greatest emphasis on the adult in their mediating or scaffolding role. The second criticism is that no recognition of the child's **emotional experience** of learning is evident. The importance of joy, fear, frustration and their effects on motivation receive no attention. However, you will discover in other sections many theories that have built upon Vygotsky's work but that have a very different approach.

7. Cognitivist Theory

It's generally agreed that psychology involves the study of cognitive processes: thinking, emotions, behaviour and perception. The chapters on the work of Piaget and Vygotsky showed the development of cognitive psychology, and this chapter summarizes some important ideas from two other leading 20th-century cognitive psychology theorists: Jerome Bruner and Noam Chomsky.

Bruner's and Chomsky's work focused initially on the mental processes of reflection, logical reasoning, problem-solving, planning and recall, and then later on the cognition involved in social behaviour, emotion and perception. This work is grounded in the idea that human beings are involved in doing activities, and these involve particular, **activity-related knowledge**. Therefore, the research and theory has targeted the processes of thought and behaviour that are intrinsic to the activity and related knowledge. Cognitivists reject the behaviourist idea of humans as relatively simple biological organisms that interact with their environment in a stimulus–response manner. Instead, they have focused on the person as **active** and **purposeful** in their thinking and behaviour, and a great deal of sophisticated experimentation and theory has resulted.

Jerome Bruner

Bruner (b. 1915) is an American psychologist, whose earliest work in the mid-20th century was mainly with adults. However, he developed his ideas into an entire theory of cognitive development, with a special focus on the role of language, communication and education. Bruner thought, like Vygotsky, that children's involvement with more knowledgeable and mature adults was key to the processes of learning, and he also placed the ability to learn as central to human intelligence. He was much less in agreement with Piaget's staged theory of development and the whole idea of 'readiness' for different learning and developmental challenges. Bruner believed that children's learning took place gradually with the support of more knowledgeable others:

> *The idea of 'readiness' is a mischievous half-truth. It is a half-truth largely because it turns out that one teaches readiness or provides opportunities for its nurture, one does not simply wait for it.*
>
> Jerome Bruner

He also had little time for psychoanalytic theories with their emphasis on inner drives and the unconscious. He was interested in the social and cultural influences, the task or activity, and the interactions between people. Two types of knowledge were identified in Bruner's work: **factual knowledge** and **procedural knowledge**, in other words, the *what* and the *how* of any activity. He argued that for any

47

cognitive processes such as thinking, comparing, classifying, or choosing to take place, the individual has to have some ideas about the nature of the thing with which they are involved, and also how to go about understanding and dealing with this thing. For example, even in infants as young as three months, it's possible for them to have enough knowledge of faces, and of their mother's face in particular, for them to distinguish and recognize the latter.

 Observe or imagine a toddler during their first-ever visit to a zoo. It's likely that they have never seen a tiger or lion in real life. It's also likely that they have seen a domestic cat. On first seeing the 'big cat' they are very likely to communicate that they recognize it as a cat and make meowing sounds, or ask to stroke it. They have not been taught about animal classification and they have no prior knowledge about lions and tigers, and yet they're making sense of them in a way that highlights the distinct human quality of reasoning and categorizing.

 Key ideas from Bruner

- The result of a child's cognitive development is the increased capacity to think.

- As the child matures and has more experience of the world, s/he finds ways or systems of organizing this experience and knowledge. Bruner called these 'generic coding systems'.
- These generic coding systems are an example of procedural knowledge, i.e. the *how to learn* knowing rather than the *what is learnt or to learn* type of knowing.
- Bruner believed that each individual had to go beyond the existing ways of teaching and learning and create their own ways of grouping, understanding and problem-solving. For Bruner, this was the essence of intelligence.
- Bruner placed great importance on **language** in the process of cognitive development and he recognized that language was a product of the society and culture into which the individual was born.
- Language, along with other 'culturally invented technologies' such as information and communication technology, helped the individual use and develop their capacities to make sense of the world.
- Even very young children are intelligent and active in their sense-making and learning about the world.

According to Bruner, the typical three-year-old will have a much greater understanding, knowledge and skill in relation to books than a twelve-month-old. Because they have been read to on many occasions, perhaps visited the library or been shopping with their parents and bought books, they will understand that books contain stories, that the marks that make letters and words can be looked at and then spoken, and that they tell a story or give information. They will have some understanding that there's a particular way to hold a book and turn the pages, as they are likely to have seen their parents or others reading. In terms of cognitive theory, they will have had enough experience of books to be able to organize this experience and recognize a book and book-reading. They have grouped and organized their experience and are in a position to use this knowledge in a problem-solving way. So when they are given a new book, although they may not have seen this particular book before and cannot yet read, they have enough **procedural knowledge**, unlike a much younger child, to make sense of the book and its purpose.

If you give a twelve-month-old a picture book, how might they behave? Will the child hold the book the right way up, turn the pages from front to back, look from the top of the page to the bottom, know that there's a story, or that the pictures have something to do with the story? Or will they hold the book the wrong way up, not know how to turn the pages, mouth and chew the book, maybe even crunch or tear the paper? Compare their response with another child of three years, who is attending pre-school and who has reached the stage of cognitive development that allows him or her to have a much better understanding and knowledge of books and how they work in general.

Another important part of Bruner's theory was his classification of three main ways in which knowledge or information about the world was stored or memorized by the individual. He called these classifications **modes of representation**. The first is **enactive representation**, and this is the type of knowing that arises from and is embedded in doing or action. The knowledge is stored as a kind of memory in the physical body. For example, riding a bicycle is usually known from actually doing the bike-riding. Children and many adults would struggle to put the many complex aspects into words and to describe it exactly.

The second is **iconic representation**, which is all about visual memory and visualization. People vary in the degree to which they can create and use mental pictures. The simple idea of individual learning styles suggests that people have different ways of learning, and this includes some being visual learners. Although learning style theories have been criticized as being far too simplistic, there's no doubt that some people do find learning through visual presentation, such as tables and diagrams, alongside verbal information, tremendously helpful.

The third type of representation is **symbolic representation**, the last to develop according to Bruner, in which information is translated and stored in symbolic or code form. This form of representation is the most useful and far-ranging for, unlike actions and images, symbols such as words or mathematical symbols like numbers can be used to represent large and diverse types and amounts of information about the world. The child who can call *all* books a book, rather than one particular book only, has a much greater capacity to communicate and to learn. In the same way, for example, if the child can use the language symbol 'cat', he can then group together, organize and use information about a large number of feline organisms.

Imagine that a child of reception age is being taught about number. In what order, according to Bruner's modes of representation, should the following learning activities be made available?

- Pictures of different amounts of food items with the numbers marked on posters in the home corner of the classroom.
- Mathematics work sheets involving numbers only.
- Number songs involving counting on fingers.
- Colouring-in sheets featuring objects alongside the number of objects presented.
- An addition test.

- Play dough cake modelling with an adult counting out the cakes.
- Playground counting games marked on the playground surface, such as hopscotch.

Bruner's ideas suggest that when a new learning activity is embarked upon, it's helpful if his three modes of representation are considered so that the learner, child or adult, begins with enactive, then iconic and finally symbolic presentation of learning materials. This obviously means that the way in which new learning is presented, and the work of the teacher, are very important aspects of the individual's learning; but it also suggests that even very young children can be helped in a constructive and active manner.

Noam Chomsky

The son of Russian immigrants, Chomsky, born in 1928 in America, was responsible for moving the focus of linguistics from the production of language, i.e. vocabulary and speech production, to the much deeper concepts of linguistic knowledge. Like Bruner, he rejected behaviourism in relation to understanding language development. He was profoundly aware of the need to make sense of cognitive development in relation to social and cultural aspects of human intelligence. He made it clear that language did not arise from the storage of huge amounts of vocabulary or as a stimulus–response behaviour. Instead, he argued that language was constantly created *spontaneously* in relation to activity in the world. Humans, therefore, had to have the capacity to use whichever words they heard in completely new combinations and to then create sentences and phrases never heard before in a particular situation.

Chomsky is known for a number of key ideas including the **language acquisition device** and **universal grammar**. He believed that children's language development could be explained through their understanding and acquisition of grammar. He thought that there were two main aspects of language: firstly the surface structure, which is the speech that children hear from adults; and secondly the deep structure, which is the complex system that organizes the way in which words are used meaningfully. Chomsky argued that the speed at which children grasped this deep structure and also operated proficiently at the surface level, without being formally or consistently taught by more language-proficient and articulate adults, demonstrated that children across the world, distinct from the young of any other species, must be born equipped with the capacity to generate language. Chomsky named this capacity the 'language acquisition device', and he thought that it had some basis in the brain. The language acquisition device made it possible for children to tune into, learn and use the 'universal grammar' that underpinned the language of their birth context.

Adults are often amused and surprised by the child's capacity to use language and to come up with some original expressions. You can observe Chomsky's language acquisition device and universal grammar ideas in the speech of any young children. I know one little girl whose very first words were: 'I want acupoftea.' She was barely a year old and there's no way she could have been taught the use of verbs ('want'), object ('acupoftea') and personal pronouns ('I'), and yet she produced this utterance to the amazement of her just waking parents at an appropriate and meaningful time, early one weekend morning. Take some time to listen to any very young child and observe how skilfully and creatively they learn and use language.

Although Chomsky's work has been criticized for being overly 'mentalist' – with too great an emphasis on the innate capacities of individuals and not enough acknowledgement of external factors – many of his ideas are very useful in thinking about questions such as the basis for language, for being human, and also the concept of critical periods for learning. Chomsky's notion of a universal grammar has also been criticized, as language structures around the world have been increasingly identified as more diverse than his theory acknowledged. Returning to Bruner, he actually blended Chomsky's ideas with his own and came up with the term **language acquisition support system**.

This allows for the social-interaction aspects of children's language and cognitive development and highlights the many ways in which skilled language-users, i.e. adults, support children in parenting, caring and educating roles.

Cognitivist theory has produced a number of ideas that have proved useful and effective, particularly in schools and education in general.

The key ideas

- The focus of cognitivist theory is on the mental *processes* of reflection, logical reasoning, problem-solving, planning and recall, and not the brain structures and nervous system involved.
- In recent decades this focus has moved also to cognition involved in social behaviour, emotion and perception.
- Bruner's ideas place the role of language, communication and education as central to cognitive development and human intelligence.
- Bruner's key terms: factual and procedural knowledge; enactive, iconic and symbolic representation.
- Chomsky, like Bruner, saw humans as active learners in a particular social-cultural context.
- Key terms for Chomsky include the generative theory of language development, universal grammar, and the language acquisition device.

---

8. Information-Processing Theory

As with many of the theories covered in previous chapters, the following psychological theories aren't specific to children's psychology, but they are described here because they have contributed some important ideas and are frequently drawn upon in the work of child psychologists.

The previous chapter on cognitivist psychology described how the mental processes involved in planning, learning, problem-solving, thinking and recall were the focus of study. Information-processing theories have the same focus but use different models or representations to understand people's cognition. Over time, depending on the technologies available, people have likened the brain and nervous system to a clock, a steam engine, a telephone switchboard, a central heating system, and more recently a computer. Basically, information-processing theories see the person as a mechanism or system that receives information and then makes use of this in a way that is evident in their subsequent behaviour.

It follows, then, that the person's cognitive system involves many complex processes including those aspects involved in thinking, language and memory. In information-processing terms, the individual must be able to:

1. Receive information
2. Understand information

3. Organize and process information (categorize, create rules, use symbols)
4. Recall information
5. Use information.

If all of the above criteria are met, the person should be able to learn and their behaviour will reflect this. If they have reached the stage of being able to understand and express themselves in language, then obviously it will be easier to gauge all of this; and if they have not, as the parent of any pre-verbal child will know, it will be a lot harder.

 According to information-processing models of human learning, the behaviour of a child should result from the information they have been given. For example, if you tell your toddler that the radiator is hot and will hurt them, in information-processing terms there are a number of questions to be asked about the child's cognitive development. Put the questions about the child's cognition (learning and understanding) in the second column in their logical order to match the questions in the first column:

Can the child:	
1. Receive information?	A. Can they use the information and not touch the next radiator they meet?
2. Understand information?	B. Can the child organize the information that radiators are hot, along with other hot things they have experienced?
3. Organize and process information?	C. Can the child understand what 'hot' and 'radiator' means?
4. Recall information?	D. When they next meet a radiator, can they draw on this stored information and remember it?
5. Use information?	E. Can the child listen and receive advice/instruction?

Answers

1 – E
2 – C
3 – B
4 – D
5 – A

This is a very simple illustration of a complex process. In reality, the stages described above would take some time and lots of repetition and, in behaviourist terms, reinforcement. You might also observe the child making sense of the fact that radiators can be hot and can hurt through their play and their drawings. A child's drawings are another example of the human capacity to organize, process and represent information about the world, in the same way that adult art forms work. In Chapter 23 you can read a little more about the use of art-based approaches with children.

Much information-processing theory has developed as a result of the work of **Alan Turing**. He was a British mathematician whose work on artificial intelligence systems, what we now call computers, was famously used in his Second World War code-breaking of the German 'Enigma' coding machine. Turing managed, through working out the rule systems involved, to gain access to German strategy and made an enormous contribution to the outcome of the war, as well as to later information-processing theories of human cognition.

The idea that human cognition was also rule-governed (see point 3 in the criteria for effective cognition, above) and could be replicated in sophisticated computers has been useful in much further research by others such as Herbert Simon, Allen Newell, Marvin Minsky and John Searle. Simon and Newell spent decades designing computer programs that could problem-solve like humans. Their work was very theoretical and abstract and by-passed philosophical and sociological issues such as what it was to be a person, the nature of knowing, and the effects of culture and social structures. However, Minsky addressed this to some extent and laid the foundations of new ways of thinking about human cognition that highlighted the networks and connections across the brain and nervous system rather than the fixed structures. Searle's work took this further by proving that people were capable of making sense and creating rules, and rules about rules, to deal with information they had never been exposed to before, and for this reason were much more complex than any computer could be. Nevertheless, despite these limitations, the information-processing theories have proved to be important in understanding and researching huge areas of human psychology such as memory, language and learning.

The key ideas

- Information-processing theories see the person as a mechanism or system, e.g. a computer.
- In information-processing terms, human cognition involves receiving, understanding, organizing and processing, recalling and using information.
- Being able to make and use rules and symbols is key to cognition.

- Social and cultural factors influence the rules and symbols available to people.
- Computers deal with information and have limited capacities to create it. The very best computer in the world is only as good as the person or people who created it.
- People are more complicated and more original than computers.

---

9. Neuropsychology

Neuropsychology: The study of changes in behaviour that result from alteration in the physical state of the brain.
Fontana Dictionary of Modern Thought

Strictly speaking, neuropsychology can't be described as a cognitive theory, but it's placed in this section as it seems to be the best fit. Neuropsychology is a highly specialist area of psychology that has a particular focus on the structures and processes of the brain and nervous system and their relationship with behaviour. A large amount of research is being undertaken, and the theory base is growing all the time. Psychologists, including child psychologists, are using the knowledge coming from this area more and more. Through being clear about the part of the brain where damage, disease and/or disorder has occurred, it's possible to make treatment and intervention more effective. Also, patterns and types of behaviour can highlight particular brain damage. In addition to this, aspects of learning, development, teaching and childcare are benefiting from the deeper understanding that neuropsychology offers.

The idea that particular behaviours and skills are organized and controlled by specific parts of the brain is not a new one. During the period from the mid-18th to 19th centuries, physicians and anatomists developed something called phrenology, which literally means reading of an individual's character from examining the shape of the skull. Different parts of the skull were assigned different roles and functions; so, for example, one area might be assigned to speech, and the manner in which a person used speech could be read from the shape and size of the bump in that area.

Modern neuropsychology has moved a long way from the idea of assessing a person's character and intellect from bumps on the head, but the basic idea that regions of the brain are the site of various complex processes such as perception, memory, language, reasoning, motor skill and emotion is very much a key aspect of the theory.

Research on the brain is difficult for many reasons, the simplest of which is that the brain is not only fundamental to staying alive but is responsible for controlling and ensuring the major processes of the entire person, mind and body. If the research in any way affects the incredibly fine balance maintained by the work of the brain, the person will be altered, possibly in harmful ways, irreversibly.

Early research, involving surgical removal and examination of parts of the brain, relied on opportunities that arose from people who had experienced brain injury. This was followed by much finer surgical exploration and the use of electrical stimulation of small areas of the brain, usually with animals. Since this time, many very sophisticated and relatively risk-free procedures have been developed using micro- and laser-surgery, MRI scans and ultrasound.

Information-processing theory has also played a part through the development of simulated brain processes and advanced mathematical models.

Discoveries about the brain's structures and processes seem to be reported in the popular media on a daily basis. Claims about the location of the basis or cause of all sorts of issues and conditions such as dyslexia, dyscalculia, dyspraxia, and attention deficit hyperactivity disorder (ADHD) are reported. The problem with all of this is that while there's much to be gained from advancing our knowledge of the brain and nervous system, it can be simplified to a virtually meaningless extent. However, child psychologists are increasingly making use of the growing knowledge base. Their use of neuropsychological assessment methods and materials appears to be increasing for a wide range of childhood disorders, injuries and illnesses. In time, and as this work grows, it should be easier to usefully communicate the key ideas and what continues to be learnt to non-specialists and the general public.

The key ideas

- Neuropsychology is the study of the structures of the brain and nervous system and the relationship between these and behaviour, including children's development and learning.

- It has long been thought that particular behaviours and skills are organized and controlled by specific parts of the brain.
- Theories of neuropsychology state that particular regions in the brain are responsible for various complex processes such as perception, memory, language, reasoning and motor skill.
- Neuropsychological research has developed through the use of many very sophisticated and relatively risk-free procedures for examining the brain.
- Neuropsychological assessment methods and materials appear to be increasing for a wide range of childhood disorders, injuries and illnesses. Much is still to be learnt.

PSYCHOANALYTICAL THEORY

10. Freud

*Analytic experience has convinced us of the complete
truth of the common assertion that the child is
psychologically father of the man and that the events of
its first years are of paramount importance for its whole
subsequent life.*

Sigmund Freud

Sigmund Freud (1856–1939) emphasized the importance of the very early life of the child and the relationship between the child and parents. He viewed the quality and health of this relationship as a crucial part of the foundations for ongoing development and future adult behaviour, cognition and overall well-being. Although not always directly attributed to him by later researchers and theorists, vast areas of child psychology have developed from his work and from this core idea that early experience is of fundamental importance. At the start of this book, four main theoretical approaches were described: behaviourism, cognitivism, humanism and psychoanalytic (also known as psychodynamic) theory. Freud is generally credited with being the founding father of psychodynamic theory, which in therapeutic practice is usually described as **psychoanalysis**.

Sigmund Freud

The links between psychodynamic theory and behaviourism are evident in this quote from Freud:

> *The reason why the infant in arms wants to perceive the presence of its mother is only because it already knows by experience that she satisfies all of its needs without delay.*

This stark view of the relationship between baby and mother reveals Freud's very traditional medical and biological background and the dominant behaviourist model of human behaviour of the time when he started to develop his ideas in the late 19th and early 20th centuries. Children were viewed as complex organisms with basic drives for food and shelter, and Freud developed his psychodynamic theory on the basis that as the child matured and formed relationships with significant others, its 'drives', or instincts, became more complex and were predominantly of a sexual nature. He extended these ideas further to propose a theory of society and the social world in general.

> *Our civilization is entirely based upon the suppression of instincts.*
>
> Freud

Unsurprisingly, many of Freud's ideas met with resistance, and nowhere more so than in his native Vienna.

Interestingly, psychodynamic theory was initially accepted more readily in the USA and in Britain. The very word 'resistance' links directly with Freudian theory, and its use in explaining people's rejection of Freud's own thinking illustrates the compelling and pervasive nature of his ideas. Freud, when challenged by any criticism of his theory, is said to have responded that this was merely a defensive reaction against the truth of his ideas. Although Freudian theory has been heavily criticized by the academic community, his ideas continue to bloom in the therapeutic practice of many psychotherapists, and it's commonplace to hear terms originating from Freud's work in everyday language. In the table below are a number of terms that you may well use yourself.

Key words and phrases arising from Freudian theory

Projection	Part of an individual's armoury of psychological defences, in which they unconsciously deny their own thoughts and emotions and attribute these to another person.
Separation anxiety	The intense fear experienced by the young child when separated from the key person to whom they are emotionally connected.
Free association	The spontaneous and unforced utterances of patients receiving psychoanalysis that reveal their innermost wishes and motivations.

Object	The person or thing needed for emotional relief and satisfaction.
Oedipus complex	An idea from Greek mythology in which the boy or girl romantically views their opposite-gender parent as a love object and has murderous thoughts about their same-gender parent.
Fixation	An aspect of the unconscious mental processes of an individual, in which all psychic energies and actions are intensely focused on a thing or person.
Psychosomatic	The manifestation of mental distress in physical symptoms.
Repression	The rejection of desires, motivations and/or fantasies, and the unconscious refusal to act on them, because the person feels that to gain satisfaction in this way would be psychologically harmful and/or risk disapproval from others.
Freudian slip	The exposure of someone's unconscious thoughts or desires through utterance or humour.

Freud believed that as the infant matured s/he increasingly experienced emotional ups and downs and felt the need for love and other strong desires. He also placed great importance on the physical aspects of the child's development and the child's innate drive to experience pleasure through different parts of the body at different ages. Freud linked these with phases of psychosexual development – **oral**, **anal**, **phallic** and **genital** – and the corresponding types of gratification behaviours included sucking, defecating and masturbation. The table below outlines the stages, the psychosexual development phases, and the typical behaviours that normal children and adults experience, according to Freud.

Birth, during weaning, pre-school	Oral	Preoccupation with food and drink, sucking and chewing.
Toilet training and early childhood	Anal	Preoccupation with toilet and bowel and bladder functions.
Middle years of schooling	Latent period	A period of no particular bodily or sexual focus.
Puberty	Phallic	A focus on gratification of emerging and increasingly conscious sexual desires, usually via masturbation.
Post-adolescence, adulthood	Genital	Participation in mutual and adult sexual relationship.

This staged theory of psychosexual development was extended further, and individuals who experienced less than ideal conditions at certain points were viewed as being 'stuck' at the corresponding stage. The stage at which the individual was 'stuck' was then employed to characterize and describe disordered personality development. For example, an 'oral-passive' person, who has been weaned too late, tends to be dependent on others and enjoy oral gratification like eating or smoking. An 'oral-aggressive person', however, will have been weaned too early and will display aggressive behaviour and tend to chew on pencils or finger nails, etc. 'Anal-aggressive' people, whose potty training was slow, according to Freudian theory are over-the-top socially, excessively friendly or aggressive. 'Anal-retentive' types, who had very strict toilet training, are mean and perfectionist in their behaviour and outlook. A major problem with Freud's theories is that they have been popularized to such an extent that the complexity and sophistication of his ideas has been replaced by very crude and loose ways of describing human behaviour, to a ridiculous and unhelpful degree. Describing a whole and complex person as 'anal' or 'phallic' on the basis of casual observation – and, most likely, a less than ideal interaction – is obviously not the same as hours and hours of professional in-depth psychoanalysis!

Actually, the dilution of Freud's ideas is only one of the many criticisms of his work. A range of other major objections have been levelled against them, and these explain the continuing strong ambivalence of the academic community to Freudian theory.

Major criticisms of Freudian theory

- Most of Freud's theory developed from his clinical practice, i.e. single cases, and could not be replicated and tested further.
- Freud's professional history is littered with many conflicts and fractured working alliances.
- Many claim that his professional practice was conducted in a way that was not ethical. For example, he treated his own daughter and subsequently wrote about this in support of his theories.
- Freud placed enormous significance and importance on human sexual behaviour. Many subsequent theorists and practitioners consider this to be an unhealthy and distorted exaggeration, which represents an artificial division between relationship and physical sex.

Freud's **Oedipus complex** theory of children's psychosexual development suggests that every very young child entertains romantic thoughts and desires about their opposite-gender parent, and also destructive and murderous thoughts and wishes about their same-gender parent. For example, a very small boy, according to Freud, will love his mother in such a way that he wishes to replace the father in his mother's affections and even destroy the father in order to achieve this. As the boy matures, he resolves this largely unconscious wish through identifying more and more with his father and renouncing his mother, to the point where he can find his own sexual partner. Freud believed that most very young children are bisexual and that their development as sexual adults expressed their own unique mixture of female and male characteristics and the effects of the primary relationship with their parents. Modern theories of human development highlight many other factors and processes as being important, such as:

- Parental behaviour and lifestyle
- Relationships with other involved adults such as relatives, friends and carers
- Family history and patterns of adult sexuality and expectations
- The local and national context and culture
- The media.

Spend a day thinking about and observing your young child and their exposure to the media. Jot down the programmes they watch or the music they listen to and then sum up what sort of things they have learnt about adult relationships. Now decide if what they viewed or listened to reflects exactly what you try to teach them.

The key points

- The earliest life of the child and her/his relationship with parents is crucially important to development of character, behaviour and cognitive styles.

- Most people grow up with strong emotional issues that affect thoughts and behaviour at an unconscious level. It may become necessary to face and resolve these issues in order to get on with normal, functional adult life.

- Most people use defence mechanisms to avoid having to face their deepest and most difficult beliefs and motivations and to keep them at an unconscious level.

- Freud placed enormous emphasis on the sex drive but later psychoanalytical theory recognizes and addresses a much broader range of human emotional and cognitive experience.

The effects of Freud's work have been far-reaching, and this is evident in the way that people use his terminology and ideas on an everyday basis. It's not difficult to find some of his ideas very appealing and relevant – for example, who could argue with the following sentiment?

All that matters is love and work.

Freud

In fact, his ideas are so dominant in mainstream culture that many people mistakenly consider these to represent the main body of psychological theory and practice today. Most psychologists would be pleased to get a pound for every social occasion when a non-psychologist quipped: 'Oh no, are you going to analyse me?' It's therefore ironic that a large proportion of the professional psychology community holds such strong reservations about his work. Nonetheless, a book on child psychology would be incomplete without some explanation of his theory and the implications for understanding child development. In addition, Freud's work, and later the work of his daughter Anna, laid the foundations for another important body of theory called 'Attachment Theory', about which the next chapter is concerned.

11. Theories of child and parent relationship, including Attachment Theory

The young child's hunger for his mother's love and presence is as great as his hunger for food …

John Bowlby

The importance of the quality of the relationship between infant and parent/s, which Freud's work highlighted, has been developed in a number of key theories of child development. One of the best known and used is the major theory of social development called **attachment theory**. Anna, Freud's youngest child, who never gained formal medical or psychological qualifications but who became an eminent child psychoanalyst working with psychologically disturbed children, developed her father's adult-based work through her treatment and close observation of children in the Hampstead War Nurseries, which she set up with her close friend Dorothy Burlingham. Like most complex psychological theories, attachment theory was explored and re-formulated over time and many researchers, theorists and practitioners contributed to the massive and ever-growing literature and related theory as we know it today. Key names include Melanie Klein, John Bowlby and Mary

Ainsworth and, later, Donald Winnicott. This chapter will summarize some of their most important ideas.

Melanie Klein

Melanie Klein (1882–1960) psychoanalysed young children through play-based techniques. From her interpretations of the ways in which individual children played, she formed an understanding of the child's fantasies about their own bodies and also their parents' bodies. She became especially interested in depressive illness and the links with Freud's 'oral' stage of psychosexual development. From this emerged her ideas about the centrality of the relationship between the feeding mother and infant to all of the baby's subsequent relationships. The main beliefs of the Kleinian psychoanalytical school that grew from this work, known as the **object-relations** school, are that:

1. Analysis should focus on the emotional bonds and behaviours within two-person relationships and the individual's attempts to balance love and care for another with that of oneself.

2. Kleinians believe that infant development occurs in two stages. The first is labelled the **paranoid-schizoid position**, and this dramatic term refers to the infant's psychological survival techniques for dealing with their innate fantasies about death and destruction in their quest to separate from the mother. The second stage is called the **depressive position**, which the child enters

as s/he becomes able to see her/his mother, 'the object' of his/her affections, as a separate person. Her/his energies are focused on retaining her love and care while at the same time dealing with the ongoing fantasies of rejection and anger.

When a baby is born, so too is a parent. However, the huge needs of an infant can evoke some strong emotions and emotional needs in the mother or father, which can then make them feel helpless and vulnerable if they are not cared for and supported themselves. When you became a new parent, what helped you to feel resilient and strong enough to cope with your baby's many needs? Think of the emotional, physical and social support that made the difference, and think of what would have helped even more.

Donald Winnicott

Donald Winnicott (1896–1971), a paediatrician and psychoanalyst, built on earlier key ideas about child development. His work is also associated with the 'object-relations' school of psychoanalysis. He too, highlighted the fundamental importance of parenting and the two-way nature of parent and infant interactions. He proposed that four main aspects of the child's development were supported and affected by these interactions:

- Social understanding and behaviour
- Capacity for relationship
- Language acquisition
- Awareness and use of emotions.

Winnicott viewed the psychological problems of children and adults as arising from poor and insensitive parenting, and based treatment around the idea that therapy should help the person to re-create and heal their earliest parenting experiences.

Winnicott is known for two particularly important theoretical ideas: the **transition object** and the **good enough mother**. Winnicott's studies of mothers and their babies and small children produced a particular explanation of how children achieved their own separate identities. He believed that the mother initially had two central roles and functions: she was both the infant's first environment and also his/her object.

The precursor of the mirror is the mother's face.

Winnicott

In Winnicott's view, as the baby gradually matures the mother becomes a separate person for the child. She helps this process by providing for his/her needs but also giving the child space and freedom to make choices and express wishes and needs, not always in line with her own choices and wishes. Very importantly, being human, she also shows that she can sometimes be fallible and/or not completely perfect in doing everything in the way that the baby wants things done. This is the idea behind the phrase, 'the good enough mother', and it's an important idea for ensuring that the child's expectations aren't always met and that s/he has the opportunity to develop greater tolerance of frustration and disappointment. This can be a difficult time, and anyone who has experienced the notorious 'terrible twos' stage with their toddler will recognize what Winnicott means in the following quote:

Children need more of their parents than to be loved;
they need something that carries over when they are
hated or even hateful.

Winnicott

The 'good enough mother' makes it possible for the child to have ownership and control of his very early objects, and this is where the idea of the 'transitional object' originates, for many small children have a special possession, such as a blanket, soft toy or dummy, that they seek out, to which they are especially attached and which is fairly indispensable. In Winnicott's theory, the object has special emotional and psychological significance and provides emotional comfort and a sense of continuity and identity. Gradually, as the child grows older and experiences more of the world and is able to make more choices and relationships, the object loses its significance and its presence is usually no longer necessary.

 Attachment theory maintains that the emotional, psychological, social and overall well-being of the child is dependent on the quality of their relationship with their key carer/s. The ideal relationship should feature sensitivity to the child's needs and feelings and should be constant and reliable.

John Bowlby (1907–90)

Bowlby's many years of clinical practice with children who were separated from their mothers formed the basis of his major book, *Separation and Loss*, published in 1969, and the initial formulation of attachment theory. Bowlby had repeatedly observed the primary need of small children for closeness and comfort from their parent, and he discovered how this need was expressed through the child's early behaviours such as crying, babbling, smiling and grasping. This need exists in its own right, separate from core needs such as satisfaction of hunger and thirst and for safety and shelter. He underlined the fact that the child was active in seeking out the parent's nurturance and affection and that this was a key characteristic of psychological health and well-being in normal child development. For those young children unfortunate enough to have to undergo long periods of separation or even loss of their parent, some clear stages of response could be discerned through the child's behaviour. These stages were firstly protest, then despair and finally detachment. Bowlby is responsible for the term **maternal deprivation**, to which he refers in *Separation and Loss*:

> [A]n infant or young child should experience a warm, intimate and continuous relationship with his mother or permanent mother substitute – one person who steadily mothers him – a state of affairs in which a child does not have this relationship is termed 'maternal deprivation'.
>
> Bowlby

The problem with Bowlby's work and the concept of 'maternal deprivation', however, is that the idea tended to be used too generally and was offered as an easy explanation for developmental problems, including disturbed behaviour. Nevertheless, it did form the basis of further work and a more refined understanding of children's complex socio-psychological development.

In our culture children tend to be brought up by one or two key figures during their very early years. It's therefore a big wrench when the child has to experience separation from their parent or carer, even if it's for a short time and they are left with familiar, alternative temporary carers in a known place. Can you think of an occasion when you have had to leave your small child? Can you recognize the stages of protest, despair and detachment? It's easy to make sense of the protest and despair that a young child can express through their behaviour and expression, but the detachment behaviour can be harder to understand. For example, on your return you would usually expect the child to be pleased to see you and to express this by seeking immediate contact, but it can often be the case that you get the cold shoulder treatment and are ignored, and your expressions of pleasure and affection can even be rejected. Attachment theory provides a useful way of understanding this situation, and the wise parent will give the child time and space to get used to their renewed presence and not actually feel rejected and rebuffed.

Some distressing research on children in Romanian orphanages has highlighted Bowlby's early ideas in stark detail. Many of the very young children, separated from their parents on a permanent basis, demonstrated a degree of detachment that prevented them from engaging in anything other than the most basic survival behaviours, such as eating, drinking, toileting and sleep. The development of social behaviour, physical play, language and overall development were all seriously delayed. Of course, the orphanage studies highlight not only the effects of separation from primary carers but also the after-effects of serious trauma, and the effects of a particular type of institutional care.

The fact that large numbers of the Romanian orphans have been adopted by replacement carers and then made great developmental progress, shows the resilience of children and their capacity to recover and to re-engage with the usual developmental processes. This has also contributed to a better awareness of the factors and arrangements that can reduce the effects of early separation and loss, such as a familiar and adequately resourced care environment, familiarity with alternative carer/s and, if possible, reduced length of separation.

KEY TERM

Attachment behaviour is behaviour that allows the child/person to achieve proximity to another, more competent person in relation to existence in the world, and that is present within an **attachment relationship**, which features:

1. Active seeking of the attachment figure.
2. Expression of anxiety and/or anger when the attachment figure is absent.
3. Confident exploration of the environment in the presence of an attachment figure.

Phases of attachment behaviour

The infant will respond to any adult who addresses core needs, and disturbances in behaviour are largely due to environmental irritations and/or shortcomings.	Birth to three months
Begins to select and actively seek key adults. Behaviours can include cooing, smiling, grasping, putting arms up.	Up to and beyond six months
Stranger anxiety. Can discriminate between key adults and others and express fear or pleasure in relation to these. The beginnings of mobility, i.e. crawling towards or away from key carer.	Six months to a year
Development of language and social awareness. Seeks and initiates social interaction for its own sake, not just in relation to satisfaction of core needs.	One year plus

Much of the development of attachment theory has happened as a result of Mary Ainsworth's work. Ainsworth (1913–99) came up with ways of measuring and assessing the quality of children's attachment. One of the most famous methods was her **strange situation** test, in which an infant of between six and twelve months is separated briefly from their mother eight times. The infant's response to their mother on her return is observed and assessed after each episode, and the child is then classified according to three broad attachment types: securely attached; insecure-avoidant type; and insecure ambivalent/resistant type, with further classifications within these categories. This test has proved useful in assessing children's well-being in different care situations, although it has been criticized for not taking cultural or social aspects of the child's usual upbringing into account and is quite brief and limited.

Many professionals involved with the care and health of children use attachment theory a great deal. However, strong criticisms do exist. A major problem is that it can be used in a crude and over-generalizing fashion to support the political and economic ends of government. The idea that all problems in an individual's psychological develop-ment can be attributed to the quality of their mothering experience doesn't take into account a host of other fac-tors and influences such as the physical and social resources available – that is, other caring and key adults, the place and culture of the child's early years, and possible biologi-cal, innate characteristics of the child.

Three major modifications to attachment theory are generally accepted these days:

1. That the age-related stages of attachment are better thought of as sensitive periods that can vary according to the child and the social and cultural context.
2. That more than one key attachment figure, usually the mother, is possible.
3. That later strong relationships and emotional experi-ences throughout life contribute to the individual's psy-chosocial development.

The third point is evident in the contribution of Donald Winnicott's ideas to the work of psychotherapists. In their work, therapists seek to re-create the qualities of the early ideal mother-and-infant relationship as a way of healing older children and adults and forming psychological well-being and health. In essence, this ideal relationship offers love and playfulness, something Winnicott referred to as a 'play space', in combination with encouragement to be independent and self-aware.

Key points from Attachment Theory

- The first and core relationship a child has is with his/her parent, usually the mother).
- This first relationship is the template for all subsequent relationships throughout life, and is central to the child's emotional, psychological, social and overall well-being.
- The quality of the attachment between child and parent is important for the child's understanding of social interactions and situations, capacity for relationship, language and emotional development.
- The quality of this first relationship should feature sensitivity to the child's needs and be constant and reliable.
- Assessing and understanding the child's attachment and related behaviour, relative to their age, can be used as the basis for therapeutic treatment.

- Development of the theory suggests that not just the mother can be an attachment figure, that 'good enough' parenting is key, and relationships throughout life contribute to psychological health and well-being.

12. Lifespan Psychology

Eric Erikson, born at the turn of the 20th century, was an American developmental psychologist of Danish/German origin who undertook psychoanalytical training and is best known for his staged model of lifelong human **psychosocial** or **personality** development. This rich theory is placed in this section because of Erikson's background, his use of Freudian ideas and his emphasis on the emotional and relational aspects of human development. His major work, *Childhood and Society*, was published in 1950, and in this he lays out the core ideas for this way of understanding the major challenges and growth points that each person encounters throughout life.

Erikson had some strong and hopeful ideas about childhood:

> *It is human to have a long childhood; it is civilized to have an even longer childhood.*
>
> Erikson

He saw the individual's earliest years as key to their lifelong development and well-being, and believed that this development happened in broad age-related stages that built on the previous stage and led to the next. At the same time he recognized that children were resilient and capable of having less than perfect lives and of learning from their experiences:

> Children 'fall apart' repeatedly, and unlike Humpty Dumpty, grow together again.
>
> Erikson

He also saw the structures of family and society as fundamental to ensuring the capacity of the child's progress towards psychological well-being and maturity:

> Defenceless as babies are, they have mothers at their command, families to protect the mothers, societies to support the structure of families, and traditions to give a cultural continuity to systems of tending and training.
>
> Erikson

As this is a book on child psychology, we will explore the five stages Erikson theorized that infants, children and teenagers have to pass through. However, the remaining four stages of adulthood and older age are also worth reading about, as, according to Lifespan Theory, the psychosocial development and well-being of adults is key to ensuring the same for children.

The first of Erikson's stages is that of infancy, the period from birth to about eighteen months to two years of age. This is the stage of life characterized by dependency on carers and the beginnings of complex psychological development, e.g. thought, language, movement and social learning. The key psychosocial developmental challenge for an infant is that relating to **trust** and **mistrust**. Ideally the baby or toddler will learn that they can trust their main carers, who in most respects represent and actually *are* their world, to provide for all of their needs, keep them safe, and to be loved. However, for infants who do not experience these, then mistrust can develop.

Have you ever observed a baby who has started to crawl, and who shows obvious fear about something that doesn't actually warrant this? This child has learnt, in some way, that the situation and/or activity is not to be trusted. Some previous experience has taught them to mistrust. Can you think analytically about what may have happened to the child previously, exactly how it is affecting them now, and what they need in the future to develop more appropriate levels of trust?

The second stage centres upon later infancy/early childhood, i.e. about eighteen months to two to three years. The key psychosocial challenges of this age relate to **autonomy** and **shame/doubt**. During this phase the child is becoming more and more able with bodily needs such as toileting and also with physical movement in general. This equips him or her to be active in exploring and experiencing the world. This can be a tough time for both child and parent, and the phrase 'terrible twos' captures the battle of wills that can result. Parents who safely and reasonably support their child's explorations and choices will allow the child to develop increasing levels of choice and expression and increased autonomy, but insensitive and controlling parents can instil a sense of shame and doubt.

It's dinner time. Your two-year-old is sitting at the table along with you and perhaps another parent/carer. You have prepared everyone's favourite, for example, roast chicken and roast potatoes. Along with this are carrots, sweetcorn and peas and some gravy. How do you ensure that your child eats well but has some say and exercises some choice, in what and how much they eat?

You might try putting a small amount of each food on the child's plate and doing the same with your own food. Discuss the different tastes, textures and appearance of the food. Talk about how the food was prepared and where it came from. Ask what they like the best, and talk about your own preferences and why it's important to eat even a small amount of different food types. If your child expresses a preference for one particular type of food, offer more when everything has been eaten. Try to make mealtimes as relaxed, consistent and sociable as possible. It's important that everyone, including the cook, enjoys this time.

The third stage extends from early childhood, about three years, up to formal school age of about five years. Motor and cognitive skills continue to develop and imagination starts to be expressed, usually in play and drawings, most obviously. In general, the child's active curiosity and wish for exploration of the world is evident. Erikson's challenge for this stage involves **initiative versus guilt**. The best parenting will recognize and support the child in an age-appropriate and safe way and foster initiative, but parents who damp down the enthusiasm and are critical of the youngster's imagination can contribute to the child feeling guilty.

 Your four-year-old has an imaginary friend with whom they play and talk, usually when they are on their own. Psychologists have found that this is not an unusual occurrence and is actually a helpful and transitory phase of cognitive, social and emotional development. It's important to accept the child's initiative in creating this playmate and in no way to make them feel ashamed or guilty or unusual. If the child refers to 'their friend', it's probably best to acknowledge and accept their 'playmate' but also to keep things real by letting them know that you know this is 'pretend' and part of their play.

The fourth stage covers from about six to eleven years of age, the primary or elementary stage of schooling. This is a time when the skills of literacy and numeracy are acquired, and the child mixes more and more with people outside the home, learning about their society and the culture in which they live. Achievement and increasing levels of self-control are hallmarks of this time, and Erikson described the major challenges as **industry versus inferiority**. Parents and educators should aim to ensure that the child experiences their efforts as worthwhile and engaging; if they don't, it's likely that the child will have feelings of unworthiness or even inferiority to others.

The phrase 'catching them being good' is worth remembering at all times, but for the child of six to eleven it's important not only to catch but to comment on the good behaviour. If you have a child of this age, make a point of noticing when they make a real effort, work hard or behave really well, and reflect it back to them. Be specific, use 'I' noticed/heard/saw you do the noteworthy action and express pleasure and pride. You don't have to give a material reward, but the child is likely to feel rewarded nonetheless by your positive feedback. This will motivate their natural tendency to be industrious and to experience good feelings about themself.

The fifth and final stage is that of adolescence, typically a complicated time for most young people and their families. This lasts between eight and ten years, starting at about ten to twelve years of age and lasting until early adulthood.

Marked physical growth, sexual development and the push for independence, choice and privacy increases. Erikson considered the main themes of psychosocial development to be **identity versus identity confusion**. Young people of this age have to discover who they are, what they want to do and be, and where they fit in the world. It's probably true to say that many people get stuck at this stage for some time – and not unusually, well beyond the early twenties. Ideally the young person will be supported in exploring different options, given increasing freedom of choice and a strong, supportive family base.

Remember when you were a teenager? Not many people forget because it's often a time of strong emotions, risk-taking and confused relationships. Can you write a letter to your young self from your adult self? Can you express what you were feeling, what and who was important to you, and what you would like by way of support and information? You will find this is a rich exercise, and what you learn is well worth keeping in mind if you have adolescent children of your own now.

Erikson's first five stages of psychosocial development

Ages	General developmental challenges	Psychosocial challenge
1. Infancy: birth – 18/24 months	Dependency; early development of thought, language, movement and social learning.	Trust and mistrust (HOPE)
2. Later infancy/early childhood: 18 months – 2/3 years	Increasingly able with bodily needs, i.e. toileting, physical activity and exploratory behaviour.	Autonomy and shame/doubt (WILL)
3. Early childhood: 3–5 years (start of school)	Motor and cognitive skills continue to develop, and imagination, curiosity develop.	Initiative versus guilt (PURPOSE)
4. Middle & late childhood: 6–11 years	Literacy and numeracy skills develop, and the child's social and cultural experience increases; achievement and increasing levels of self-control are sought.	Industry versus inferiority (COMPETENCE)
5. Adolescence: 10/12–20/22 years	Marked physical growth and sexual development; seeking independence, choice and privacy increases.	Identity versus identity confusion (FIDELITY)

REMEMBER THIS!!!

Key points from Erikson's Lifespan Theory

- All humans develop throughout their lives.
- Each person passes through certain age-related stages of psychosocial development.
- Each stage of development presents a particular challenge, which relates to particular core issues common to people of a certain stage of life.
- This development occurs within a person's social and relational context and situation.
- The psychologically functional individual enters each developmental stage, learns and develops new understandings, ways of being and interacting with others and living, and greater psychosocial well-being, and can then engage with the next stage.
- Some people can find some stages and their related challenges particularly difficult and can become stuck and require therapeutic input and support to meet the challenges.

13. Personal Construct (Kellyian) Theory

This is a chapter that was hard to place. It could easily have been put into the cognitivist section, because the focus of this theory is certainly that of a person's cognitions. However, I decided to place it with psychoanalytical theories, since Kelly, the creator of Personal Construct Theory (PCT), was trained as a psychoanalyst and his work was very much created for use in therapeutic work with individuals.

Personal construct psychology is often referred to as Kellyian psychology after George Alexander Kelly (1905–67), the American psychologist whose prolific career contributed this rich seam of theory and applied psychology. Like many of the key figures in psychology, his work was not initially received with great enthusiasm in his home country, but developed overseas. In Kelly's case, innovative psychologists in the UK, such as Dom Bannister and Faye Fransella, have built on the core ideas and many psychologists have used these in their work with children, young people and adults.

> *Behaviour is a man's way of changing his circumstances, not proof that he has submitted to them.*
>
> George Kelly

Kelly believed, like other cognitivists, that it's most useful to work with the psychology of individuals and to see people as active and reasoned in living their lives. He was critical of the trend in 'scientific psychology' to concentrate on measurement and controlled experimentation and the reliance on statistically-based generalizations about trends in large populations. Instead, he thought it was most appropriate to explore the cognitive processes of individuals as a way to make sense of their thinking and behaviour. Kelly's theory is based on the philosophical position known as **Constructive Alternativism**, which features the following core ideas:

1. People exist in a real world.
2. All elements and processes in the world are inter-connected.
3. The relationships between these different aspects are in constant motion and interaction.
4. Each individual has a unique, personal and infinitely variable experience and view of this world.

 As your child grows and becomes more able to communicate their constructs (ways of making sense) about the world, you will hear more and more about their unique viewpoint. Take, for example, the beginning of school. Children from the same family, the same age, the same socio-cultural background, or any number of shared situations will have very *different* expectations and experiences, and in the earliest days they may express these very clearly. Can you compare what your child said about their first experiences of school with another child's comments and descriptions? In what ways were they similar, and how were they different?

Theories of child psychology, such as Piaget's staged theory or Freud's psychosexual development theory, maintain that every child goes through the same phases at roughly the same ages. However, Personal Construct Theory, with its focus on individual sense-making, would argue that there's an infinite variety of personal experience and ways of making sense of this, and that the important thing is not what stage the child is at; rather it's the quality of being listened to and understood that matters. In this way, a parent can most effectively be supportive, reassuring or actively helpful.

Kelly, whose main work took place in the two decades before his early death at the age of 62, did not live long enough to develop his personal construct psychology with children specifically. However, others including British educational psychologists Phillida Salmon and Tom Ravenette have begun this process. Salmon has written about the relevance of Personal Construct Theory, because it offers a way of understanding adults who work with or care for children, and ultimately an insight into children's learning and early construct-making.

A very important idea from Kelly is that each person bases their behaviour and way of being in the world on a set of personal constructs: a **personal construct system**. These constructs, unique to the person, are more complex than beliefs or rules, and they are constantly changing and adapting to what we learn from our experiences. They have been described as cognitive 'templates' or 'lenses' through which the individual experiences life, and upon which the person bases their behaviour and predicts what is likely to result from their behavioural choices.

> *Constructs are essentially predictive. Thus when we construe a man as honest rather than dishonest we are essentially predicting that if we lend him money we will get it back. ... It is precisely because our constructs are predictors that our construct systems are in a continual state of change for each of us.*
>
> Don Bannister

Each person's behaviour is the observable expression of their constructs in different situations at different times. Following from this is the possibility that if the person can be helped to be aware of their constructs, they can be active and creative in making adjustments and developing more effective behaviours in order to achieve psychological health and well-being and to live life most fully and effectively. Clearly this is likely to be of benefit to parents and their children, for there are an infinite number of approaches to the complex work of parenting, and Personal Construct Theory can be very useful in helping individuals and families to find the way that is right for them.

The 'elicitation of constructs' exercise

Ask yourself the question: How would I describe a good parent? Allow yourself only three descriptive words or phrases as answers, and be spontaneous in your reply. Just say what comes into your mind. Now that you have the three words or phrases, ask yourself what would a parent be like who did not have each quality or characteristic? For example, you might say that a good parent was 'caring' and that the parent who was not 'caring' was 'callous', 'cold', 'hard', etc. I could go on but this might influence your responses, and the point being made here, above all else, is that the replies that you make are a reflection of *your* personal construct system in relation to parents/parenting.

You'll see this for yourself if you try the exercise with other parents. The chances of people coming up with the same descriptors are remarkably slim. Certainly there may be some similarities, but the exact words and phrases aren't likely to be the same for any two people. A construct always has two aspects: the **emergent pole**, the first aspect to be expressed, such as 'caring'; and the **contrast pole**, the aspect that sums up what is not the emergent pole, such as 'cold'. This makes the construct: caring/cold.

It's possible to have some very useful conversations about the construct, and many techniques, of which you will read more later, have been created to structure these conversations and to explore the construct.

The exercise you have just done illustrates Kelly's idea of **man as scientist**. For Kelly, each individual's behaviour could be likened to an experiment in which his or her construct system is tested in the world in a continuous problem-solving manner. He stated very strongly that making sense of actions and interactions was not just for psychologists:

> *Abstraction and generalization of human activity are not the exclusive prerogatives of professional psychologists. What they do any person may do. Indeed every person does! Each individual the psychologists study abstracts and generalizes on his own for he is even more vitally interested than they can ever be in the task of understanding himself and his relationship to other persons and values.*

> George Kelly

Many sophisticated interviewing and therapy techniques and approaches for face-to-face work, and even computer programs, have been developed. Central to all of them is the usefulness of the question, which is, as Tom Ravenette wrote, 'the bridge between two people: a subtle and delicate means of two-way communication.'

The 'elicitation of constructs' exercise above is a simple example of one technique for understanding an individual's thinking and behaviour. Using the example of the caring/cold construct about parenting, here's another technique. **Hinkle's Ladder** is an approach in which, once some constructs been have elicited, the person is questioned in more depth about why it's important to be one aspect of the construct, i.e. caring or cold. Below is an example of a personal construct psychologist using this technique with a parent:

Personal Construct Psychologist (PCP): 'So when I asked you about how a good parent could be described, you said they should be caring rather than cold. Can you tell me why it's important to be caring?'

Parent: 'It's important to be caring as a parent because the child will feel secure.'

PCP: 'How would you describe a child that is not secure?'

Parent: 'Clingy, not able to cope unless they were helped and encouraged all the time.'

PCP: 'So which would you choose, a secure child or a clingy one?

Parent: 'Well, secure, I guess.'

PCP: 'Why is it important for the child to be secure?'

Parent: 'They would be more independent.'

PCP: 'So what would a child be like who is not independent.'

Parent: 'Soft and needy.'

PCP: 'And which would you choose: independent or soft and needy?'

Parent: 'Well, actually, I suppose I might choose soft and needy.'

PCP: 'Why is it important for the child to be soft and needy?'

Parent: 'So that they need their parent and the parent is special for them.'

PCP: 'So what would a child be like who doesn't need their
parent and doesn't see them as special?'
Parent: 'They would go to anyone, not just the parent.'

This example, which is entirely fictional, shows just how
complicated a person's construct system can be – and how
contradictions and ambiguities often feature.

---

1. Choose one of the words/phrases you
thought of that describes a good parent.
2. Make a grid like the one opposite and write your word/
phrase in the space marked **A**, e.g. 'caring parent'.
3. Now put into the space marked **B** your word or phrase
for what a parent would be like who wasn't at all **A**, e.g.
'cold parent'.
4. Next decide why it's important to be **A** and put your
word/s into the grid marked **C**, e.g. 'secure child'.
5. Now describe the contrast for **C** and put this word/
phrase, e.g. 'clingy child needing reassurance', in **D**.
6. Choose between **C** and **D** and describe why it's important to be that one. In the example above, it's <u>**C**</u> and the
word that describes why it's important is 'independent'.
This is placed in the box **E**, above the preferred aspect
of the construct, i.e. <u>**C**</u>. E is not underlined because it's
not the chosen side of the construct. In each case, the
chosen pole of the construct is underlined.

7. Describe the contrast for **E** and put this into **F**.
8. Choose between **E** and **F** and describe why it's important to be that one. **F** is underlined because it's the preferred side of the construct and not E.
9. Whichever pole you choose, put your word/words in the box above the chosen one. In the example this is **G**. You will notice that at this point you have switched to a different side of the grid layout. This changing sides is an important point in the process of trying to understand the individual's construct system.
10. Describe the contrast for **G** and put this into **H**.

And so on …

H (e.g. A CHILD WHO WILL GO TO ANYONE)	<u>**G**</u> (e.g. THE PARENT IS SPECIAL AND NEEDED BY THE CHILD)
E (e.g. INDEPENDENT CHILD)	<u>**F**</u> (e.g. SOFT & NEEDY CHILD)
<u>**C**</u> (e.g. SECURE CHILD)	**D** (e.g. CLINGY CHILD NEEDING REASSURANCE)
<u>**A**</u> (e.g. CARING PARENT)	**B** (e.g. COLD PARENT)

This is quite a complicated process, which is why working with a skilled personal construct practitioner, often a professional psychologist, is preferable to doing it on your own. It's important to ask pertinent and genuinely open questions, to move through the process systematically, and also to make careful and thorough notes.

This in-depth questioning can go on for some time. In the above example it's becoming clear what is important to this parent. Look at the grid that sums up this dialogue. It stops at an interesting point in the exercise, because in this imaginary example the parent is beginning to see some benefits to their child being less independent, and if the conversation went on they might say: 'Because the child is only little and I, the parent, need to be needed!' It really depends on the age and development or particular needs of the child, on the parent's own history of being a child and/or experience of being a parent, on the family and social traditions and many other factors. This example shows how, by exploring the person's constructs and the deeper meanings behind them, a great deal of useful information can be gained; and from this, some changed thinking and behaviour can develop. It also shows very clearly how intertwined the needs of the parent and child actually are!

As already stated, conversations like this are best done within a framework of professional practice, and only if the person whose constructs are being explored wishes to explore them. However, you might like to try it out privately by thinking about one of your own constructs and questioning yourself in this way.

Personal Construct Theory is not without its critics, who say that the problem with focusing on the psychology of individuals is that it's labour-intensive, i.e. there aren't enough psychologists and therapists to work with everyone who might benefit. Also, it's not feasible to generalize or to address large-scale social issues. Kelly didn't theorize about the idea of universal constructs, i.e. constructs held by groups, organizations or entire populations, although he did consider that patterns or themes of similar meaning-making existed in groups. PCT is a theory that, by definition, is in a state of constant change and development, so it's likely that some interesting ideas and ways of working are yet to come.

Key points about PCT

- George Kelly created Personal Construct Theory, and based his ideas on Constructive Alternativism, a view of the world as being ever-changing, interactive and real, experienced in unique and personal ways by individuals.
- PCT offers a way of exploring the cognitive processes of individuals in order to make sense of their thinking and behaviour.

- Each person has their own set of personal constructs – a personal construct system. These constructs, unique to the person, are more complex than beliefs or rules, and they are constantly changing and adapting to what we learn from our experiences.
- In PCT, understanding *how* and *why* individuals make sense of their experiences is more important than stages of development.
- Everyone is a scientist about themselves, and each person is constantly experimenting with their own behaviour as a way of testing their personal construct systems.

BEHAVIOURISM

14. Pavlov's Classical Conditioning Theory

The behaviourist sweeps aside all medieval conceptions. He drops from his scientific vocabulary all subjective terms such as sensation, perception, image, desire, and even thinking and emotion.

J.B. Watson

In the late 19th century, the earliest psychology was based on the belief that human beings were distinct from all other living creatures because humans possessed consciousness and were therefore different and more complex than animals. In 1913 John B. Watson (1878–1958) created a completely new theory called **behaviourism**, in which he maintained that the study of people's mental processes should be abandoned in favour of a focus on their observable, and preferably measurable, behaviour. Watson was not only interested in constructing a grand theory; he considered that psychology should ultimately concentrate on 'the control and prediction' of behaviour. Watson's behaviourism was based on the following key ideas:

1. Thoughts, emotions, wishes and expectations, i.e. 'mentalist' processes, do not determine or explain what people do,
2. Behaviour results from conditioning, i.e. experience in the world.
3. For a behaviourist, learning is simply the acquisition of new behaviour as a result of environmental experience.
4. Humans are essentially biological organisms.
5. Humans do not consciously act, they react to experiences and conditions in their day-to-day lives.

These ideas support the behaviourist view that the understanding and control of human behaviour can be gained from studying animals' behaviour. Early behaviourist studies are therefore well known for experiments involving animals such as dogs, rats and birds. Although Watson's earliest work was met with great criticism, for he was challenging some established philosophical and religious beliefs of the time, behaviourist theory developed and became central to much English and American psychology of the early 20th century.

The criticisms have continued, the main one being that human behaviour and the human social world are far too complex to be compared to animals, and that laboratory experiments using animals that concentrate on physiological aspects and ignore inner processes and the possibility of people being active and responsible, are too simplistic and artificial. However, behaviourism has established the importance of the scientific study of behaviour in psychology, and many very useful approaches and techniques have resulted. This chapter will look at these ideas through exploration of the work of key contributors.

Ivan Pavlov

Pavlov (1849–1936) was born in Russia and as a young child suffered a serious injury; as a result he spent much of his childhood with his parents in the family home and garden, developing a range of practical skills and a strong interest in natural history. He became passionately interested in science and the possibility of using science to improve and transform society. He studied medicine at university and learnt directly from a famous physiologist of the time about the nervous system. Years of neurophysiological experiments with animals followed, and Pavlov became more and more convinced that human behaviour could be understood and explained best in **physiological** (physical and biological) terms rather than in 'mentalist' terms (inner processes of thinking and/or feeling).

The experiments for which Pavlov is best known are those in which he used the feeding of dogs to demonstrate a number of his key ideas. In these experiments, just before feeding, a bell was rung. Pavlov found a way of collecting and measuring the dogs' saliva production when they heard the bell, and he discovered that once the dogs had been trained to associate the sound of the bell with food, they would produce saliva, whether or not food followed. This showed that the dogs' physical response (salivation) was directly related to the stimulus of the bell, and the saliva production was therefore a **stimulus response**. The continued increased salivation, even when the dog had experienced hearing the bell without any food following, was a **conditioned reflex**. This whole process is an example of **classical conditioning**, and it always involves a physical and spontaneous response to certain conditions that the organism has learnt by association. Behaviourist theory has used these ideas in explaining human behaviour.

As the following quote illustrates, Pavlov would argue that the child's nervous system and general physiology is conditioned to require the satisfaction of biological needs.

It is obvious that the different kinds of habits based on training, education and discipline of any sort are nothing but a long chain of conditioned reflexes.

Pavlov

For example, a child may anticipate a certain food and their appetite and eating behaviour will be dependent upon that item. What do you think?

The vast majority of popular parenting and child-care advice stresses the need for a familiar routine. This links with the behaviourist principle that humans, like other animals, have biological needs, which must be satisfied regularly and consistently for overall well-being. Daily life with young children is generally made a lot easier if some of the basics like eating, drinking, washing, dressing and using the toilet are done in a routine way. Some routines are so implicit that you can be barely conscious of them until the routine is broken and for some reason you do things differently. Try thinking of an occasion when you had to change one of these routines and consider the effects. For example, you may have got into the habit of giving your child a particular food for breakfast, and one day you found that you had run out of this product. How did the child respond? What behaviours did they present? Did they eat as much as usual, and did they need any special encouragement or help to eat?

15. Skinner's Instrumental/ Operant Conditioning Theory

B.F. Skinner (1904–90), an American psychologist, based his work on the principle that only the links between observable behaviour and the stimuli from the outside world could be used in a scientific psychological understanding of behaviour and learning especially. He developed the ideas of Pavlov through his own experimental work with animals and is best known for his theory of **operant conditioning** (see below). He disagreed with Watson's earlier ideas that private experiences, thoughts and emotions were outside the range of behaviourist theory, arguing that the conditioning process could apply as much to private as to public behaviour.

Skinner exemplified his ideas through the way he lived generally. For example, he constructed a crib for his baby daughter that was designed to offer a constant, controlled and balanced physical environment, highlighting his rather clinical perspective on optimal child development. His reaction to a school report for one of his children, saying that she lacked motivation, was that in fact what was lacking was reinforcement from the teaching staff!

Skinner had some ambitious plans for applying his theory to education. Using the ideas from operant conditioning, he devised a 'teaching machine'. This machine would be programmed to impart knowledge to the pupil who, when he successfully learnt the unit of knowledge, was duly rewarded. Surprisingly, this idea caught on to the extent that substantial amounts of public money were invested in its development. But, not surprisingly, it was found in practice to have limited effectiveness. The age-old problems of what should be taught and how this 'agreed knowledge' should be communicated were never addressed, and Skinner's teaching machine, in his words, was extinguished.

Skinner's emphasis on the power and control of whoever is in charge of the living or learning context is evident in all of his experiments. He is best known for a number of studies with rats and birds, where different creatures were trained to respond in certain ways through the use of deprivation or reward. In his earliest experiments with rats, he tried to answer the question of which conditions in the animal's environment could be manipulated in order to shape aspects of the many types of rat behaviour. He used a range of equipment but is well known for the mazes in which he placed rats. In brief, parts of these mazes contained food and the rat could access these parts only if it pressed certain bars. He also created boxes in which he placed pigeons, and much like the rat mazes, these 'Skinner boxes' as they were known, contained food pellets. The pigeon could get the food only if it pecked at levers that would then release a pellet. He found that the pigeon would continue to peck in the way that released food for some time after food was actually available, but after a period of fruitless pecking, what he called the **extinction period**, the bird would give up. So, in this way, by manipulating the pigeon's environment, i.e. making food available or withdrawing it, he could either **condition** or **extinguish** the behaviour. Skinner identified and named the four phases of behaviour involved in this **operant conditioning response** as **deprivation**, **satiation**, **conditioning** and **extinction**.

 Think back to when your child was very young. Think of an occasion when they wanted something that you were sure they shouldn't have, for example, a bar of chocolate. The point at which they attempted to get the chocolate can be called the deprivation stage. At this stage, many small children will try a number of different behaviours in order to get the object of their desire. They might reach towards it, demand, cry or try to snatch it from you directly. You might then let them know that if they don't just grab it, and sit quietly, you will reward them with a small piece. If you're able to maintain this strategy and reward their behaviour consistently, they will eventually become satiated and will probably get bored and seek some other activity or, in behaviourist terms, **stimulation**. On the next occasion they will hopefully have learnt what they need to do to get some chocolate, and in Skinnerian terms, will have become **conditioned** so that they don't even attempt the crying, demanding and snatching and will wait, even if they don't get the chocolate every time. However, this period of conditioned behaviour will last only so long before the behaviour becomes extinguished and the old behaviours – and possibly some new ones, like sneaking the sweet while you aren't looking – will emerge.

Behaviourist theory developed from animal experimentation rather than direct studies of human behaviour because human behaviour and the human social world are just too complicated to replicate realistically and to control, which is crucial to the tests carried out in order to develop behaviourist theory. There are also major ethical aspects to consider, such as possible harm and threats to psychological and physical well-being of humans, and this is why it wouldn't be a good idea to try Skinner's radical behaviourism ideas in their pure form with children. However, there's no doubt that behaviourist ideas have been used to great effect in supporting the development and learning of children.

In my work as an educational psychologist I have seen many education professionals, especially those involved in the management of children's behaviour, using these ideas. You are almost certain to have seen them in use in the popular parenting television programmes. Consider the use of star charts, for example. This system of monitoring and rewarding children's behaviours depends on being able to break the child's behaviour down into easily observed and recorded behaviours. It's also essential that the desired behaviour is very clearly described to the child and that they realize that when they demonstrate this and, hopefully, it's noticed, they will be rewarded with a star. The strategy can be extended even further, and if the child is old enough to understand and to be able to wait, they can be told that a bigger, more meaningful reward such as a special treat will be given to them when they have earnt a certain number of stars. In other words, their desired behaviour is acknowledged and celebrated and they are motivated or conditioned to do more of it. The 'naughty step' is another way of working with children's behaviour, but the idea here is to extinguish undesirable behaviour. If, for example, the child in the example above keeps taking chocolate without permission, they are taken to a designated step on the stairs and made to sit there for a set amount of time, separate from everyone else and with no access to rewarding activities.

Can you think of some aspect of your own adult behaviour that you do because you're rewarded for it? Can you think of some aspect of your own adult behaviour that you don't do because to do so would incur punishment? Many of the framework of rules and laws within which we live in modern-day society can be seen as fulfilling the principles of Skinner's operant conditioning, but at the same time the theory doesn't address all aspects of human life. Look at the list that follows and decide whether behaviourist theory adequately addresses these questions.

- Can human behaviour be organized and observed accurately in measurable units?
- How can different people's value systems and beliefs be taken into account in making sense of their behaviour?
- What part does individual conscience play in their choice of behaviours?
- What part do larger social organizations and culture play in the individual's behaviour?
- Can the person or persons in powerful positions that affect the context for the behaviour always be trusted to do what's best?
- How long can a person, and especially a child, be deprived of something they want and remain hopeful, and not just give up?
- Can the neuropsychological aspects, i.e. brain structures, be completely ignored in understanding and controlling behaviour?

Your answers to these questions are likely to be very similar to the major criticisms of behaviourism. However, it's important to acknowledge the contribution of the theory's key ideas about systematically observing behaviour and using the knowledge gained to help address problematic behaviour and to promote positive behaviour.

Let's now look briefly at some approaches, loosely described as **behaviour modification** methods, that have their basis in behaviourist theory, making particular use of Skinner's ideas. Behaviour modification has been used in many different forms with some success in helping children and young people to develop more desirable and constructive behaviour in school and home situations.

In the first instance, very systematic observation and analysis of particular behaviour is required. In its most rigorous form this is known as **Applied Behavioural Analysis** (ABA) and is generally a method that only a professional, often a psychologist, would be expected to use. Certainly, parents or teachers have far too many other things to concentrate on, and they can't offer the level of detachment, objectivity and precision required for this in its pure form.

Once the specific behaviour requiring modification is identified, it's then possible to create a schedule to achieve it. This will inevitably feature goals, records of progress and evaluation and rewards. Star charts, as I mentioned before, have become the order of the day for many television parenting programmes and have mixed, often short-term success, but they do embody these aspects of behaviour modification programmes. In schools, teachers have used all sorts of rewards such as house points, team points, golden time, free choice and individual and class treats. Most teachers recognize the limited usefulness of external rewards for good behaviour and aim, over time, for the child to find their better behaviour so much more intrinsically rewarding that this is reward enough. Ideally, programmes should be set up with children and young people that involve them actually setting their own targets and goals, monitoring and recording their progress and then selecting the rewards that are meaningful for them personally.

Take your imaginary child at the time when they are in their mid-teens. Choose an aspect of their lifestyle that they would really like to change. It may be taking up a new type of physical activity, a hobby or a stress management activity. The emphasis is upon *taking up* rather than *giving up*! Firstly, pretend that you're their life coach and have the young person spend a week just observing and recording how they spend their spare time. Next, identify what they could choose to substitute with the new lifestyle behaviour. Set some targets. These should be SMART, i.e. **specific**, **measurable**, **achievable**, **realistic** and **timed**. Maybe they would like to take up running. In the first instance the target should be modest, so maybe clearing a couple of short sessions a week from time spent on computer games or watching television and substituting fast walks. If this works for the first week, then short runs of a minute or two can be inserted into the walking sessions. If this works, then more of the walking time can be used for running, and then maybe another session can be undertaken each week and so on. This is an example of a behaviour modification programme that uses the principle of **self-management** and builds on success. Much simpler programmes are possible with younger children as long as the target behaviour and rewards make sense, are feasible and are meaningful to the child.

Key points about Behaviourist Theory

- The only aspects of human behaviour and thinking that are worthwhile topics for investigation and intervention, in terms of theoretical and applied psychology, are observation and measurement of behaviour.
- Behaviour results from a person's experiences in the world.
- Humans are biological organisms like other animals.
- Humans don't consciously act or make free choices, but react to the experiences in their daily lives.
- Rewarding experiences are responded to by doing more of the behaviour that has been rewarded.
- Behaviour that leads to non-rewarding experiences is ceased or reduced, i.e. extinguished.
- Behaviour modification approaches, including applied behavioural analysis, use observation, monitoring and recording, target-setting and rewards in interventions designed to change and improve behaviour.

16. Social Learning Theory

This is another theory that doesn't fit terribly well into just one section, as it's generally viewed as the bridge between behaviourist and cognitive theory. Social Learning Theory (or Social Cognitive Theory, as it's otherwise known), created by Canadian psychologist Albert Bandura, extends the view of a person's behaviour as resulting from their environmental experiences to include the part played by that person's expectations, beliefs and ideas, and the examples of behaviour provided by others, i.e. biological, cognitive and environmental factors, all in constant interaction with each other.

> *Observational learning is vital for both development and survival. Because mistakes can produce costly or even fatal consequences, the prospects for survival would be slim indeed if one could learn only by suffering the consequences of trial and error.*
>
> Albert Bandura

Bandura (b. 1925) believes that learning happens primarily as a result of watching others and imitating them. For children, especially the very young, the key models for learning are parents and carers, and children's engagement, attention, memory, and motivation are all dependent upon the social aspects of their learning. If you recall the example of the child brought up by wolves in Chapter 5, this provides a very vivid example of how so much learning and development is dependent upon the models provided by others. Vygotsky's theory is another important influence that fits with Bandura's ideas about the social nature of learning.

Modelling: The behaviour, attitudes and behavioural outcomes demonstrated by one person to another that provides an example and enables the other's learning.

Bandura's theory implies that each person's behaviour isn't necessarily an exact reflection of what the person actually knows. Can you remember an occasion when you were in a particularly testing situation, for example an interview or an examination, when you didn't show what you actually knew? You may have been feeling extremely anxious, or a bit under the weather, or perhaps you misheard or misread the questions being asked. All of these situations could have been adjusted so that you were helped to feel and function better, but because you were not, you didn't demonstrate what you were actually capable of.

Children and young people are often positioned in this way – for example, I have met many young people who underperformed during crucial school entrance examinations. Reasons have included raised anxiety because of pressure from adults, a lack of motivation because they actually wanted to go to another school to which friends were going, poor sleep, illness, problems with understanding or language, or undetected learning difficulties. I could go on …

Bandura introduced another idea that he called **reciprocal determinism**, which is the belief that not only is an individual's behaviour influenced by the social world, but the social world is affected by the person. Consider the way in which many adolescents appear to be quite loud and aggressive, especially when in groups. It's probably true to say that a strong expectation of this sort of teenager behaviour is held by many adults as well as young people, yet it would be untrue to say that each teenager is incapable of being less loud and aggressive and that there are no situations in which they show this. The power of expectations, social stereotypes and situational factors is considerable.

THINK ABOUT IT Imagine your child is given a choice of a box of Lego bricks that are all shades of pink, and a similar box that are all shades of blue. Do you think their gender would make any difference to the choice of bricks? Do you think it would make any difference if they were alone or were part of a group of other children? Do you think their age, their upbringing or the degree to which their parents engage in sexual stereotyping would make a difference?

Another term that Bandura introduced and emphasized in his theory was **observational learning**, which he maintained consisted of four stages: attention, retention, production and motivation/reinforcement. These stages are explained in more detail below.

The childhood challenge of learning and the application of social learning theory

Callum is a six-year-old who is learning to play football. His **attention** is very much brought to bear on this process because he has seen how enthusiastic his mum and dad are about people playing football, he likes the coach who comes to his school, who happens to be employed by a local football club, and his friends are very enthusiastic about the game. His coach demonstrates lots of football skills and makes sure that Callum can see close up exactly what he needs to be doing with his body to make the right moves. He also encourages Callum to watch football played by the other pupils, on the television or at the local club. **Retention** of these skills is helped through many opportunities to practise them. Also, the coach has encouraged Callum to remember some key points about various skills through verbalizing – e.g. look at where you want the ball to go, line up your foot and body, then head down and focus on kicking the ball right – and also through visualizing pictures of famous footballers playing different shots. He also encourages Callum to practise or rehearse the sequence of physical moves in his head. According to social learning theory, in the **production** stage, Callum needs to practise his new skills more and more until he can produce them quite spontaneously and smoothly. He continues to need input from his coach, especially about finer points, and gradually his feelings of confidence and ability to play football build. The fourth stage of **motivation/reinforcement** requires Callum to feel rewarded and encouraged to continue to use and practise his new football skills. His parents come to watch him play matches, and he might score a goal or make a good pass or a save and the other pupils recognize and applaud him. His coach gives him praise. Without this positive feedback he's not likely to keep practising and improving. Worse still, he may receive criticism and experience discouragement. If, for example, other pupils tease him and say he's a poor player or don't want to play with him, he's highly unlikely to persist in learning and developing as a footballer. If he sees the positive effects of playing football well, for example he notices how much high regard is given to others who play well, this will reinforce his desire and application to practise football. Eventually, if all continues well, he will experience **self-reinforcement**, and each successful experience of playing football will make him feel so good that he wants to play more and more.

The example of social learning theory in Callum's football learning illustrates the best-case scenario. Can you think of a situation when you were learning something as a child and the experience was similarly positive? Reflect on the following questions:

1. How was your **attention** first stimulated? Who encouraged you and what did they do?
2. What happened to help your **retention** of the new skills/knowledge? What did you do? What did others do?
3. In what way did you, others or the general situation support the **production** phase?
4. How was your **motivation** supported, and what made **reinforcement** happen?

It's likely that key influences on your successful learning experience included important adult figures in your life such as your parents or a favourite teacher or relative. Bandura's social learning theory places a great emphasis on the influence of adults, and his 'Bobo doll experiment' underlines this effect.

CASE STUDY

In the Bobo doll experiment, nursery-aged boys and girls were given various play experiences with adult involvement, where the type of play that the adults demonstrated either did or did not involve modelling of aggressive play. This aggressive play involved a large inflatable doll being kicked, punched and hit in the face with a toy hammer. All of the children, but especially the boys, exposed to adult models of aggressive play showed more aggression in their own play subsequently, both non-verbally and verbally. In addition, it seemed that the adult model effect of increased aggression was more marked if the child had been exposed to a same-gender adult, i.e. boys became more aggressive when they had seen adult males playing aggressively and girls more so with adult female models.

This was an important study for its time, although of course not uncriticized for aspects like the relatively small sample size of children and also an unrepresentative proportion of children from white, middle-class backgrounds. Interestingly, although Bandura's work has been described as bridging behaviourist and cognitive theory, the conclusions that he drew from the Bobo doll experiment have a distinctly psychoanalytical flavour. He considered that the increased aggression in children could be attributed to a weakening of the child's usual inhibitions of their innate aggressive impulses, as the adult behaviour models resulted in less strong social inhibitions that children are usually brought up with and encouraged to employ. In any case, the core idea from social learning difficulty is that children learn not only from the physical world but also from the social world, and their own thoughts and understanding are key.

Key points about Social Learning Theory

- Albert Bandura created Social Learning Theory as a way of bridging behaviourist and cognitive theories.
- A person's behaviour results not only from their environmental experiences but also from their expectations, beliefs and ideas, and the examples of behaviour provided by others.
- Modelling is the term describing the behaviour, attitudes and behavioural outcomes demonstrated by one person to another that provides an example and enables the other's learning.
- Reciprocal determinism is the belief that not only is an individual's behaviour influenced by the social world, but the social world is affected by the person.
- Bandura believed that children learn primarily from observational learning, which he maintained consisted of four stages: attention, retention, production and motivation/reinforcement.

HUMANISM

17. Maslow's Hierarchy of Human Needs

Humanistic psychology is often referred to as 'the third force' because many view it as following on from psycho-analytical and then behavioural theory. Key names associated with its development are Abraham Maslow, Carl Rogers and Alfred Adler. Abraham Maslow (1908–70) is usually credited with being one of the founding fathers and his major contribution was the attempt to ensure that a set of values, often described as **person-centred** principles, were employed in psychology. He was critical of psycho-analysis for its preoccupation with psychopathologies, i.e. mental health problems, and of behaviourism for being too mechanistic and too preoccupied with statistics and artificial experimentation

Maslow's ideas are captured in his **hierarchy** or **pyramid of human needs**. In essence, Maslow proposed that all people shared the same basic needs and that it should be psychology's broad aim to help people ascend further up the pyramid in order to satisfy their highest aspirations and potential for development and learning.

SELF-ACTUALIZATION
Realizing individual potential

SELF-ESTEEM
Position, responsibility and success in society

SOCIAL AND RELATIONAL
Relationships with family, friends and work colleagues

SAFETY AND WELL-BEING
Law, social rules, security

PHYSICAL AND BIOLOGICAL
Basic needs such as food and drink, shelter, rest and sleep

Maslow's Hierarchy of Human Needs

Think about the most recent day in your child's life and then, using the following headings, jot down what you have done or provided for them, according to the categories:

SELF-ACTUALIZATION
Realizing individual potential

SELF-ESTEEM
Position, responsibility and success in society/living situation

SOCIAL AND RELATIONAL *Relationships with family, friends and school mates (work colleagues)*
SAFETY AND WELL-BEING *Law, social rules, security*
PHYSICAL AND BIOLOGICAL *Basic needs such as food and drink, shelter, rest and sleep*

> *There are at least five sets of goals which we call basic needs. These are briefly, physiological safety, love, esteem, and self-actualization. In addition we are motivated by the desire to achieve or maintain the various conditions upon which these basic satisfactions rest and by certain more intellectual desires.*
>
> Abraham Maslow

Maslow believed that the focus in psychology should be on 'normal' individual human behaviour and underlying thoughts and feelings, and the higher human motivations of learning, development, social relations, ethics, morality and aesthetics.

Maslow's view of human nature and his perspective on parenting is essentially an optimistic and positive one. He maintained that if the individual's core needs are met, this will allow the person to develop in an optimal way and be able to meet each new developmental challenge most adequately.

> [I]t is precisely those individuals in whom a certain need has always been satisfied who are best equipped to tolerate deprivation of that need in the future; furthermore, those who have been deprived in the past will react to current satisfactions differently from one who has never been deprived.
>
> Maslow

A very simple example of Maslow's principle of a needs-based approach to human development is as follows:

 Freddie is a five-year-old who has just started full-time school. He has spent his early life being cared for by very loving and protective parents and his grandmother. He has had few opportunities to mix and socialize with other children because the family live in an isolated area and have few friends and no other relatives. Both mum and dad have demanding jobs, and opportunities to make friends with other parents or to take Freddie to child-based activities have been few and far between. Grandmother doesn't drive and has devoted herself entirely to keeping the home nice and caring for Freddie. Not surprisingly, when Freddie reached the age of having to go to school, he struggled.

He hadn't experienced the usual challenges of being with other children, such as having to share, to take turns, and to deal with having to wait or even go without what he wanted. All children can struggle with these challenges, but the child who has never been supported through these experiences is much less well equipped.

In the case of Freddie, although his physical, biological and safety needs have been addressed very carefully, his social and relational development is less well catered for. Unless his social experiences are broadened, for example through supporting more opportunities for play with other children, he is likely to have difficulties in the school situation that will in turn affect his self-esteem and ultimately his chances to achieve self-actualization. Hopefully, through school and home working together, Freddie's social development can be supported more effectively in order to help him develop and learn more satisfactorily. Can you think of any social activities that will help Freddie to cope better with, and learn more from, his early socialization experiences?

18. Rogerian Theory

Carl R. Rogers (1902–87), an American psychologist, built his theories from years of clinical practice. Like Maslow, he had a benign view of human nature, believing that each person's natural tendency was to interact harmoniously with the world and to learn from their experiences in order to **self-actualize**. He considered that when the person was **congruent** with (i.e. true to) and also **accepting** of themselves and their experiences, that this process was supported. He viewed the quality of care, support and **empathy** that they received throughout life, and especially during the early years, as crucial in ensuring that the person could use their experiences in a continuous and constructive process of personal development. He also proposed that these qualities should be employed by therapists in their work with clients.

 Next time you're with a close friend, think about your time together. Look out for ways in which you were able to communicate or show the following qualities:

- **Empathy**, for example: listening to and appreciating feelings and perhaps sharing your own similar experiences.

- **Acceptance**, for example: giving positive and unconditional regard and resisting the urge to be judgemental or personally critical.
- **Congruence**, for example: being honest and genuine.

Some people will immediately say that the examples above highlight the difficulties in fulfilling all three aspects. For instance, a common occurrence between friends is that one, A, asks the other, B, about their views on something such as a relationship that A has just started, or A's new hairstyle. How can you give 'unconditional regard' and yet be 'honest and genuine' at the same time? A good way to address these concerns is to start by asking yourself what you would want from a B, if you were in A's position. By being truly empathetic, congruent and accepting with yourself, you are then more likely to be like this with others.

Rogers' very positive approach extends to his view of all aspects of the living world. He believed that all creatures are designed to know what's good for them and that they are equipped to make wise choices about how to live their lives. For example, if a child gorges on a large amount of unhealthy food, he will eventually feel or even be sick. He will then stop eating this food. In the short term, this idea makes sense, but it doesn't address the fact that modern-day life makes available a large amount of unhealthy food combined with aggressive and very sophisticated advertising, which can distort the natural instincts to select good food in order to be healthy and energetic. Rogers' reply would probably be that if the adults involved in advertising, producing and supplying such foods to children were operating in an empathic, congruent and accepting relationship with themselves, this situation would correct itself. Unfortunately, the conditions for ensuring that adults have enough of a sense of self-worth that they work from this basis may not have been present in their most formative years, and so the cycle goes on – but it's never too late to try to correct this! Parenting and caring for children in a way that the parent would ideally have been brought up is perhaps one way.

Anthony is a seven-year-old who has been brought up by parents who firmly believe in Rogers' self-actualization theory of human development. As a baby and young child he was given a great deal of love and attention and all his core needs were met. He thrived and grew up healthily and happily. He was also shown a lot of **positive self-regard** from his parents and other family members and felt confident and worthwhile about being his own unique self. He would attempt to learn and achieve new skills and knowledge, carefully guided by his parents, without feeling scared of failing or feeling that he was inadequate, and if he didn't succeed initially, with his parents' support he would see this experience as giving him a better basis for trying again and would, in time, accomplish his goal. When Anthony succeeded with different developmental challenges his confidence grew and he was able to take on greater challenges. His parents would reward him modestly – sometimes, but not necessarily, with small treats – but always with their acknowledgement and expressed views of him as a worthwhile and unique person. If Anthony made demands for the sweets or toys that he saw on television or that other children might have, his parents would listen and decide in a very measured way what was reasonable and appropriate. They would try to explain their reasoning in these matters, and over time, Anthony gradually developed the same reasonable and realistic outlook and a strong sense of **unconditional self-regard**.

THINK ABOUT IT In the case example above, Anthony's parents resist the trap of only giving him positive regard 'conditionally', what Rogers calls **conditional positive regard**. All people, including children, need and are motivated to seek positive regard and affirmation of their unique selves. The principles of behaviourism, i.e. reward and conditioning, are apparent in Rogers' approach. He maintains that if individual self-regard is tied in with certain conditions, such as other people's or society's values, the person can override their natural self-actualization or inherent self-value in order to fit external conditions, which aren't necessarily in their best interest. Can you think of a time when you went against what you knew was right for you because of large-scale social or commercial pressures and standards? You can look at most areas of living for examples: relationships, food, alcohol, fashion, consumer goods. What was the effect on your self-esteem and self-regard over the long term?

Much of Rogers' work was carried out as a way of addressing the shortcomings, as he saw it, of the formal education system:

> *Our educational system is, I believe, failing to meet the*
> *real needs of our society. I have said that our schools,*
> *generally, constitute the most traditional, conservative*
> *and rigid bureaucratic institution of our time, and the*
> *institution most resistant to change.*
>
> Carl Rogers

These words, with which he begins one of his best-known books, *Freedom to Learn for the 80's*, were quite radical at the time and provoked criticism as well as approval. Many academics accused Rogers' work of lacking in validity and scientific rigour and of being too idealistic and subjective, but what Rogers had to say about the processes of and foundation for learning and the importance of **experiential learning** is worth considering, and is as applicable today as when it was written in the 1980s. Rogers' main principles for individual learning were:

- Personal involvement, that is, involvement in the learning experience of the whole person, including emotional and cognitive aspects.
- Learning should be self-initiated: there should be a strong spirit of enquiry/curiosity on the part of the learner.
- Learning should be pervasive: the learning should affect behaviour, attitudes and the entire person.
- The learning should be evaluated by the learner in terms of its personal usefulness and meaning.

 Compare your experience of learning something as an adult, e.g. learning to drive a car or use a computer, or learning about a very strong interest, with something learnt at school, e.g. an aspect of the taught curriculum such as algebra, grammar or scientific formulae, as a child. Which experience was more faithful to Rogers' principles?

---

19. Adlerian Theory

Alfred Adler (1870–1937), an influential Austrian psycho-analyst who associated with Freud during his early work, also placed education as central to individual psychological development. However, his emphasis was on the socialization of the child into wider society:

> The high degree of cooperation and social culture which man needs for his very existence demands spontaneous social effort, and the dominant purpose of education is to evoke it.
>
> Alfred Adler

Adler's **individual psychology** was based on the idea that the infant and young child experienced a state of psychological inferiority and helplessness that could be overcome only through the development of social connections, first with the parent, then the family, the school and eventually society as a whole. He saw the mother's role as essential in this process, and as a result, stressed the importance of educating parents. He also saw the understanding of other people as an indispensable aspect of healthy psychological development.

Much of Adler's work highlights the power dynamics involved in interpersonal relationships. He was one of the first to write about the very gendered aspects of social relationships and his ideas are relevant to feminist theory, developed much later. He also developed some interesting ideas about the effects of birth order or family position on psychosocial development. These have been criticized heavily for being overly simplistic and unresearched, and for not taking the multitude of other factors and influences of a child's development into account; but they are useful in that they highlight the fact that close relationships in a child's early development, other than the parental ones have some impact. Very briefly, Adler's classification of birth order effects is as follows:

Child's position in family	Effects of family position
Oldest child	This position means, by definition, that initially the child was an 'only one' who commanded all parental energy and attention. However, the loss of this special position and the added burden of younger siblings, for whom the oldest can be made responsible at times, could lead to feelings of sadness and resentment. In the worst-case scenario, Adler thought that the oldest child was most likely to experience mental health problems and/or go off the rails and engage in criminal behaviour.

Middle child	The middle child, according to Adler, was the one most likely to be successful in life, but could experience feelings of not belonging or of having to rebel.
Youngest child	Youngest children, Adler theorized, tended to be lavished with love, material benefits and attention in general. This could result in an over-inflated sense of self, selfishness and a lack of awareness of the need for give-and-take in relationships. It could also lead to under-performance and a tendency to not fulfil personal potential.

Humanistic psychology is an important strand in the vast and always growing tapestry of child psychology. It offers a way of viewing the developing child within the wider context and history of humanity as a whole. It also faces the problem of ethics and values and humanizes the science of psychology. It recognizes that psychologists are first and foremost whole, complex people themselves, albeit attempting to bring professionalism and some objectivity to bear in their work with complex psychological issues and questions. Maslow, Rogers and Adler have contributed some of the most important ideas to humanistic psychology. Let's review this section by matching the key terms and ideas to their names:

Key terms and ideas	Adler Maslow Rogers
Self-actualization – the highest drive and need for any person, throughout life	Maslow
Inferiority complex – the natural psychological state of all infants	Adler
Conditional self-regard – the person's sense of self-worth contingent on the expectations and wishes of another or others	Rogers
Hierarchy of needs relating to each person's physiological, safety, love, esteem, and self-actualization needs	Maslow
Experiential learning – initiated by the whole person who is actively involved and active in their own learning	Rogers
Empathy, acceptance and congruence – the key ingredients in any psychologically ideal, functional relationship	Rogers
Individual psychology – the psychological development of the individual based within, and dependent on, the social context in which they develop	Adler

OTHER IMPORTANT THEORIES

20. Social Psychology

Social psychology is the scientific study of social interaction. This may include interactions between individuals, within groups or organizations, or even at a societal level, and the term 'inter-personal' is applied to such interactions. It also explores the theory and research of the real or imaginary effects of these interactions on individuals. The person's thoughts or cognition, feelings and behaviour are all areas of interest for the social psychologist and can contribute a great deal to understanding the psychology of the child.

Many theoretical influences have contributed to the modern social psychology of today, for example: psycho-analytical and behaviourist theories, learning theory such as Bandura's work described in Chapter 16, and motivation theory such as that of Carol Dwek, covered below.

One central idea in social psychology, created by Prussian-born psychologist Kurt Lewin (1890–1947), is that of the person's behaviour being affected by both their own individual characteristics and the social environment, as experienced by them. Lewin came up with the following equation to explain behaviour: $B = f(P \times S)$. In other words, behaviour (**B**) is a function (**f**) of the person (**P**) and their situation (**S**). Lewin considered that the behaviour of the individual is a result of their interaction with, and within, the context in which their behaviour is produced.

Jenny is a bright, sociable eleven-year-old who has just started her new secondary school. On her first day she finds that nearly all the other children from the new intake have friends from their old schools starting with them, and many have brothers and sisters in older years. She spends a miserable first week feeling left out, lonely and increasingly stupid and confused. There's so much to learn about the school layout and timetable, and she doesn't feel that she can ask others for help because they're so busy with their friends learning about their new school. At home, Jenny's parents ask her lots of questions about school and are very enthusiastic and excited for her, so Jenny, who has always done well in everything until now, pretends all is well. Week two begins and Jenny, who has slept and eaten very poorly all weekend, complains of feeling unwell and refuses, for the first time in her life, to go to school.

TRY IT NOW! Jenny's case study is an extreme example and there are many other details that could be explored, but how would you make sense of Jenny's behaviour, using Lewin's equation? Complete columns **B**, **P** and **S** in the table below and finally complete column **f**.

B (Jenny's behaviour)	f (the reasons behind Jenny's behaviour, i.e. P x S)	P (Jenny's unique characteristics)	S (the situation)

Two examples of very well known social psychology experiments exploring social cognition and attitudes follow. The first is a study by Solomon Asch (1907–96) exploring social influences. In Asch's experiment, five students are told they are taking part in research about perception and are shown a card on which three lines of different lengths are drawn (A, B, and C on the illustration below), and then a second card on which only one line (E below) is shown. The task given to the students is to choose the line on the first card (A, B or C) that matches the line on the second card (E). Unknown to the only genuine subject, X, all other members of the group are part of the experiment and have been primed to choose C, which is obviously incorrect. Although A is obviously the longest line and C is not, X, on hearing his fellow group members, chooses C, although he can see that line A is the right answer. This study famously illustrates the effect of **social conformity** and is a key idea in understanding the effects of groups and the perceived importance of others on the individuals' behaviour.

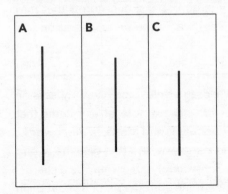

Asch's study is an important one for understanding people in most social contexts, and it has implications particularly for school contexts in which children and young people spend so much time in groups. In many ways, the group conformity effect is used to the teacher's advantage in managing large numbers of children, but the question has to be asked: at what cost to individual choice and conscience? Studies of bullying have demonstrated repeatedly the influence of 'strong' characters who lead groups of peers and exert pressure at a psychological level on individuals, both the victim/s and the bystanders, despite those individuals' beliefs and sense of right and wrong. There are numerous other examples of the effects of group influence, or in social psychology terms, **social norms** in day-to-day life. These may include social stereotypes of all kinds, for example relating to gender, race, age, disability and class. Much of modern-day educational practice works to address the powerful effects of large social group norms that may be evident in various ways, i.e. in the press, television and advertising.

 During a children's television viewing session with your child, make a note of any items that challenge your beliefs and ideals, in other words, those that feel wrong in some way and that give the wrong example to your child. For example, there may be a character who is shown as an extreme stereotype, or a situation in which undesirable behaviour is involved. Watch the whole programme and find out if the programme-makers offer any characters and behaviours or a general storyline that balances things out and offers more acceptable material for your child's viewing. Can you talk about this to your child and explain to them what you think, and also find out about their understanding? If the child was watching with a group of other children, for example in a school situation, what would you hope that the teacher would say?

Another famous social psychology experiment is the study by Stanley Milgram (1933–84) in which he explores the effects of authority. In a series of experiments, the subject, Y, was asked to assist a researcher and to administer mild, at first, and then progressively stronger electric shocks to subjects who gave wrong answers to the researcher's questions. Unbeknown to Y, the supposed subjects were, in fact, actors and no actual electric shock was administered. However, the study showed that Y and other subjects were prepared to administer electric shocks that appeared to cause acute pain to the mock subjects, even up to levels that could have been fatal. This study showed how the perception of another's authority and role, i.e. that of the researcher, resulted in people following instructions and doing things that in their usual life they would not entertain. Milgram's work was challenged and met by disbelief initially:

I am forever astonished that when lecturing on the
obedience experiments in colleges across the country,
I faced young men who were aghast at the behaviour
of the experimental subjects and proclaimed that they
would never behave in such a way, but who, in a matter
of months, were brought into the military and performed
without compunction actions that made shocking the
victim seem pallid.

Stanley Milgram

As time has passed, this work has been developed and reproduced in other contexts, such as the famous 'Zimbardo study', a piece of research carried out by Philip Zimbardo, a social psychologist based at Stanford University in the US, which looked at the psychological effects of being cast as, and role-playing, a prison officer or prisoner. The study was conducted in a mock prison on the university campus and had to be discontinued after six weeks because of the degree of distress caused to participants. As in the original study by Milgram, individuals' usual behaviour and capacity for empathy and kindness to other people was reduced and replaced with cruel and inhuman behaviours to others.

USEFUL TIP Next time you take your child to the doctor, dentist or optician, notice how they behave and compare this to their usual behaviour: for example, their willingness to sit still, listen, follow instructions, stay quiet etc. This is a situation where **legitimate**

authority resides in a particular person and the role they are fulfilling, and children usually have some understanding of this. All sorts of social interactions and situations involve rules, authority and compliance. How do you think your child develops an understanding of this?

Sometimes children receive 'mixed messages' or confusing information about authority figures. For example, if they hear a parent or carer talking disparagingly about their teacher and perhaps criticizing the teacher's work, it will reduce the teacher's standing in the child's eyes and may contribute to them being less compliant in school, or even very challenging. Another example might be a grandparent or relative who is very involved with the child allowing the child to do things that are not allowed at home, such as going to bed much later, watching television or using the computer in a way not usually permitted by the parents. Even worse, they might voice their view that the parents' rules are not appropriate, which is going to contribute to many more challenges from the child about the way in which the parents have decided to bring them up. In an ideal world, parents, relatives, teachers and all adults involved with children would communicate between themselves and come to an agreement about permissible activities and acceptable behaviour, and they would *together* work in a way that supports the legitimate authority held by adults who are key to a child's development.

Another important theory that relates to the effects of others on the behaviour of an individual is social psychologist Carol Dwek's **motivation theory**. This theory is concerned with students' **attributions** in relation to their success or failure with school work. In motivation theory, students are categorized as either 'fixed IQ' theorists or as 'untapped potential' theorists. The 'fixed IQ' attribution type of student believes that they have a certain fixed and in-born ability for academic work and can either do the work successfully and fairly easily or view trying to learn more effectively as a waste of time. Students with this kind of belief system might declare: 'I'm no good at French/science/maths or any other subject, so I might as well just give up.' The 'untapped potential' attribution type student, on the other hand, is constructive and active in their learning. If they are successful, then they put this down to their hard work and their ability. If they fail, then they see this as a reminder and an opportunity to work smarter and harder, and they will ask for help, try out different ways of studying and seek feedback on their learning.

In reality, students tend to have a mixture of attribution types, with about half veering towards the 'fixed IQ' type and the other half more of an 'untapped potential' type. When particularly challenging situations arise in their studies, such as major school change or important exams, it's possible to gauge more clearly their attribution style or beliefs about their academic success and failure. Adults can make quite a lot of difference to the way students see themselves, and can be active in helping students to plan, engage in and also evaluate their study habits. Many schools offer study support or study skills sessions, in which individual students are helped to realize their untapped potential and study most effectively.

 Remember a time when you took an examination or were evaluated in school and you didn't pass. Can you recall some of the conversations or thoughts that you had with yourself about the poor performance? With hindsight, can you imagine what would have helped at this point? Were there any key adults such as a parent, relative, family friend or teacher who could have made a difference, and if so what would they have said and/or done?

Many other fascinating studies have been carried out and theories formed within this field, and most have a direct bearing on children and young people. Especially relevant topics include attitude formation, expectancy effects such as self-fulfilling prophecies, self-concept, theory of group development and group dynamics, and inter-personal attraction. Further reading is highly recommended.

Key ideas about social psychology

- Social psychology is the scientific study of social interaction, which may include interactions between individuals, within groups or organizations, or even at a societal level, and the real or imaginary effects of these interactions on individuals.

- **B = f (P x S)** is Kurt Lewin's famous equation explaining that the behaviour of an individual is a result of their interaction with, and within, the context in which their behaviour is produced.

- The terms social conformity and social norms arose from studies of the effects of groups on individuals' attitudes and behaviour, such as Asch's line length experiment.

- Social interactions and situations are governed by rules, and in relation to this, individuals in certain roles have legitimate authority to carry out certain actions and be obeyed by others with whom they are working.

- Motivation theory is the theory that relates to students' attributions in relation to their success or failure with school work, and it can be used in helping young people to be more realistically optimistic about their capacity to make progress.

21. Ecological Systems Theory

Urie Bronfenbrenner's work emphasizes the importance of environmental influences on the child's development. Bronfenbrenner (1917–2005), an American psychologist, saw little value in studying and measuring children in anything other than their natural environments, i.e. homes, nurseries, school and the community. He also thought it was pointless to examine parenting in a way that separated the parent/s and child. In essence, he viewed children's development as a dynamic and active process in which all individuals involved influenced each other and changed over time and in relation to the contexts around them.

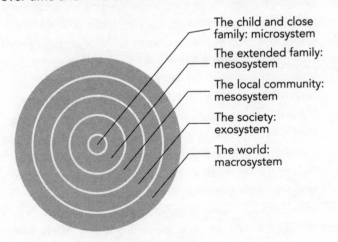

The child and close family: microsystem

The extended family: mesosystem

The local community: mesosystem

The society: exosystem

The world: macrosystem

Bronfenbrenner's model (see next page)

In **Bronfenbrenner's model**, the child and close family (the microsystem) is placed centrally to the four main social systems or environments: the extended family (mesosystem) and the local community (mesosystem); the society (exosystem); and the world as a whole (macrosystem). This is usually represented like a kind of Russian Doll so that each smaller system is surrounded and contained by a larger system.

This way of thinking about child development means taking into account a huge number of influences and factors, all of which affect the others to some degree. Below are some examples from everyday life describing those factors and influences.

The child brings his or her own characteristics, such as biological make-up, emotional disposition, cognitive ability, gender, health, current age and general developmental level; all of these make up the most immediate system, known as the **microsystem**, along with close family. For example, a child, Jane, born with a sensory impairment such as deafness is going to experience the world in a particular way that is unique to her and very different from the majority of other hearing children of her age. Jane's experiences, according to Bronfenbrenner, are affected by her deafness – but her deafness, and the way in which she interacts with others and the world at large, affects others. At a very simple level, her family and her educators will need to learn to communicate with Jane in non-auditory-based ways. Jane's pre-school and school experience, work and independent living arrangements will all be influenced.

The profound effect of the quality of the child's microsystem, i.e. close family, has been made clear from research. For example, a child's development in areas such as social skills and cognitive performance is enhanced by caring and consistent family styles. Bronfenbrenner's work, which has clarified the importance of early developmental experiences and contexts, has been key to various very large-scale government-funded early enrichment programmes for young children and their families, such as the 'Headstart' programme in the US and 'Sure Start' in the UK. The extended family into which the child is born is usually viewed as part of the next level, the **mesosystem**.

As the child ages, their involvement with the **mesosystem**, which includes school, local neighbourhood, and health services, increases. Parents know very well how important it is to find the right school, doctor and neighbourhood for their family. The school's achievement levels, discipline, inclusiveness and general atmosphere all affect how a child will progress in their formal education. A good doctor will offer an accessible and effective service for the child and the family so that if any health worries exist, these can be addressed and the family's quality of life ensured as much as possible. The neighbourhood is also key. If no parks or amenities for children and family are available, if local crime is high, then of course general well-being and life opportunities will be limited.

CASE STUDY

Steven was born in the late 1960s, in an inner-city area with high levels of crime, unemployment and poverty in general. He recalls his mother saying that she never let him out of her sight until he started secondary school. He has no memory of playing in parks as a young child or going to local shops on his own, and he was always accompanied to school. What aspects of Steven's overall development do you think will have been affected? How does it compare to your own childhood?

The friendships available to the child, and some aspects of health such as specialist services, actually belong both within the **mesosystem** and the next level, the **exosystem**. As the child grows older and attends a school or perhaps needs help from health professionals from a hospital or clinic not in their immediate neighbourhood, their context for living is widened and other influences are introduced. The exosystem is said to include family friends, neighbours, legal and social services and the media. The lifestyles, beliefs and views of other people and organizations add many new dimensions to the world in which the child is developing.

There's a common belief that many families nowadays don't have much contact with other adults, such as family friends and relatives, because of modern lifestyle choices in which people are either working or engaged in leisure pursuits that don't involve direct contact with others. In many ways the new media of 24-hour multi-channelled television, internet, social networking, mobile telephones and computer games has filled the time that was available for this in the past. There are benefits and drawbacks for everyone, but particularly children and young people, of engaging in such indirect and virtual interactions. The emotional commitment and give and take, and the possibility of building up a relationship over time and creating a deep relational history, are very unlikely in these new media. On the other hand, dealing with many different people in diverse living situations may be educative and may equip a person with a lot more knowledge (and hopefully tolerance) of people who are very different from themselves.

The last of Bronfenbrenner's systems, the **macrosystem**, is much less concrete, for it represents the attitudes, rules, ideals and traditions of the world at large. As with previous systems, some aspects of other systems overlap with this one. When you considered the effects of television, for example, on children's development, it's quite likely that you wondered about the examples of adult behaviour and the values behind these that children can view. You may have questioned the high levels of violence featured in computer games or the way women are portrayed in certain publications and television channels. All of these examples communicate strong messages to children about what adults value, what is acceptable behaviour and ways of living, and what is right and wrong and other core ideals. The macrosystem into which the child is born is much less easy to control and influence than other more immediate systems such as the family and local community, but nevertheless it has to be thought about in terms of preparing the child for life as an independent adult. Ultimately, the child's own sense of being able to make safe and wise judgements about the world at large is influenced by the ways in which she or he experiences and observes parents doing this.

 The amount of emotional support, guidance, information and practical support available to parents varies a great deal, but it's obvious that the parent who feels supported and cared for is much more likely to do the same for their children. According to Bronfenbrenner's model, such support can come from the mesosystem (extended family, local community), the exosystem (public services including health), and maybe even the macrosystem. Think about your own sources of support for parenting and list them according to Bronfenbrenner's ecological systems:

Mesosystem	
Exosystem	
Macrosystem	

It's largely true that we all share the macrosystem of the world today, and new media has meant that shared information and understanding are perhaps more possible than ever. However, the micro-, meso- and exosystems are likely to vary greatly between cultures. This was highlighted in Chapter 2 in which we explored the question, 'What is a child?', and looked at different cultural childcare practices and beliefs about childhood. Bronfenbrenner's ecological system theory offers a way of appreciating and organizing the complex social and cultural context in which every child's development takes place.

Key points about Ecological Systems Theory

- Child psychology research and applications should be conducted in the child's natural environments, i.e. homes, nurseries, school and the community.
- The environment in which a child grows up is key to the opportunities for learning and development available to them.
- A number of environments or systems affect the child's development: the child's own characteristics and close family (microsystem), extended family and the local community (mesosystem), the society (exosystem), and the world as a whole (macrosystem).

- Every environment, or system, affects and is affected by the others in different and dynamic ways.
- As the child grows, the powerful influences of home and family at microsystem and mesosystem levels are supplemented by other people encountered at exosystem and macrosystem levels.

APPLICATIONS OF
CHILD PSYCHOLOGY

22. Assessment

If a qualified psychologist, for example a chartered psychologist in the UK, is asked to work with a child or young person they will invariably start by carrying out an assessment. Sometimes this will be the entire input, and the findings and recommendations that result from the assessment will be used by others who are involved with the child on a day-to-day basis, such as parents or teachers.

Assessment should yield useful information about the child's processes of learning, social, emotional and cognitive development, and the effect of the child's living and educational contexts on all of these. The assessment can take many forms, and it's helpful to think of it as a piece of research. All research begins with a question or questions. Typical questions encountered by a psychologist working with children and young people might be:

- 'Why is my child/this pupil not making progress with their school work at the same rate as most of the other children in the class?'

- 'How can I support my child's/this pupil's language development?'
- 'What should my child/this pupil be feeling about the loss of his grandmother, and how can I help her/him?'
- 'Who can help my child to become more independent and responsible at home and school?'
- 'Does my child/this pupil need a special type of school?'
- 'How can my child/this pupil be helped to behave more appropriately at home and/or school?'
- 'Does my child have particular learning strengths or gifts, and if so, how can s/he be helped to fulfil their potential?'

The list is endless, and every individual child in their unique situation must be assessed in a way that reflects the complexity of their individuality and particular context. All assessment work should be undertaken in order to answer the question/s that gave rise to the work in a way that makes a positive difference for the child. As the last question shows, the reason for the assessment doesn't necessarily have to arise from a problem. Probably any child or adult would benefit from having access to the expertise of a chartered psychologist, who will use their knowledge and skills in a professional, objective and ethical manner to explore ways of supporting the individual's development and learning.

THINK ABOUT IT

If you were to employ a chartered psychologist for a session with your child, what questions would you like the psychologist to explore?

Although every single assessment is carried out in an individualized and creative way that is designed to take into account the complexity involved, there are nevertheless some aspects of the work that should be the same for every case. The Division of Educational and Child Psychology (DECP) of the British Psychological Society (BPS) has produced a framework of guiding principles for psychologists, which can be read on the Society's website (see References at the back of the book for details of this and other psychological associations worldwide). This document, as well as the Society's Code of Ethics and Conduct, discussed in Chapter 4, are the hallmark of professional psychology in the UK, and all chartered psychologists have a statutory responsibility to work in a way that is in line with this guidance.

Throughout this book I have emphasized the ever-changing nature of the wide range of theory available, and how psychologists have to try to keep in touch with developments, select theory carefully and appropriately, and base their practice upon this. The BPS guidance makes a very clear statement about the theoretical basis for psychological assessment of children and young people:

> *Current models of assessment need to reflect the body of psychological knowledge, which emphasizes the dynamic, interactive nature of children's learning and social behaviours within environments in which they develop.*

 If you were selecting theories on which to base applied psychology work, you would want to be sure that the theory was in line with your beliefs about children's learning. Look at the following list of people who have contributed to the creation of child psychology as we know it today, which shows to what degree these theories take into account:

1. The dynamic nature of children's learning, i.e. ever-changing, adapting and active.
2. The social nature of children's learning and the key importance of others.
3. The particular living situation and environment in and with which children develop.

Important principles about children's learning ⟶	1. The dynamic nature	2. The social nature	3. The child's particular living situation
GEORGE KELLY (Personal Construct Theory)	Yes	Yes	To some degree
SIGMUND FREUD (Psychoanalytical Theory)	To some degree	Yes	Yes
ALBERT BANDURA (Social Learning Theory)	To some degree	Yes	Somewhat
JEAN PIAGET (Piagetian Theory)	Yes	Not a great deal	Not a great deal
URIE BRONFENBRENNER (Ecological Systems Theory)	Yes	Yes	Yes

The BPS framework for psychological assessment (and intervention) emphasizes a number of points along with the need for all chartered psychologists to ensure continuing professional development and ethical practice:

1. The importance of current psychological theories and research.
2. The selection of fair, relevant, sensitive assessment instruments, methods and techniques.
3. The requirement to include information from the child's history and from different situations in which the child lives/is educated.
4. The involvement of parents and/or carers.
5. The importance of informing future plans for the child, emphasis of the child's strengths and challenges, and the child's own viewpoint as far as possible.

Other professional psychology bodies have similar guidelines, and you can find out about these through following the links given in the References.

There are many ways in which a psychological assessment can be carried out. Methods can include interviews, consultations, observation, curriculum-based assessment, applied (or functional) behavioural analysis (see Chapter 15), psychometric tests, published tests of behaviour, and social and cognitive development using checklists, ratings and questionnaire forms. The important thing is that whatever the psychologist selects should be in line with the guiding principles above, should be in no way harmful to the child's overall well-being, and should support the research being undertaken, as requested initially by the person who arranged the work, usually a parent or a teacher. A little explanation of some of these methods follows.

Interviews and consultations are usually the starting point for a psychological assessment of a child or young person. In most cases somebody (the 'client' – usually the parent/s or teacher/s) has a problem that they are hoping to solve, and so it's essential to gain as much information about their views as possible. This information will help the psychologist to choose the best methods, tests and approaches for the issues described.

The theoretical perspective of the psychologist will shape the way in which they carry out the initial interview. For example, if the approach is largely based on psycho-analytical principles, it's likely that questions will be quite open-ended, free-flowing, and designed to shed some light on unconscious aspects such as the client's feelings. A simple example might be: 'Can you tell me how this problem makes you feel, and how do you think the child feels?' Rogerian or humanist theory (Chapter 18) places great importance on the quality of the therapeutic alliance between psychologist or therapist and the client, and every effort is made to ensure that the client experiences empathy, acceptance or unconditional positive regard and congruence. The quality of listening that is made available in the interview is key to this.

THINK ABOUT IT

If you were concerned about your child, how would the following questions make you feel?

- What has led to you making this appointment?
- Describe and list in detail all aspects of the problem.
- What has gone wrong?
- What are you hoping will be different as a result of this assessment?

A psychologist using mainly behaviourist theory is likely to take a very structured approach and will want specific information, and so will be more directive and use more closed questions such as:

A. 'What has contributed and led up to this problem?'; or 'Who has been involved, where and when was the behaviour issue apparent?'

B. 'Describe the behaviour that is causing you concern'; or 'Where, when and who was involved and/or affected?'

C. 'What effects does this problem have on everyone involved?'; 'How is this behaviour having an effect, upon whom, and where and when?'

This 'ABC' or **antecedents**, **behaviour** and **consequences** approach is designed to identify the problem, the conditions and situation that have contributed to the problem, and the effects, in order to create – or as psychologists usually say, formulate – an effective intervention.

In reality, the psychologist will draw on a number of theoretical frameworks for their interview approach, but by and large you can expect more open or non-directive questions from the psychoanalytically and humanistically inclined practitioner and more structured and directive questions from a psychologist of a behaviourist persuasion.

You may be asked to complete a questionnaire prior to the assessment or at the beginning of the session. Many psychologists create their own questionnaires and inter-view schedules, but there are also a lot of published types.

Observation of children as part of a psychological assessment is a richly informative but difficult thing to do. One of the primary reasons for involving a psychologist is to gain as clear, accurate and objective a viewpoint as possible. It makes sense for many reasons to see the child in their usual contexts, i.e. home and pre-school or school. Firstly, you're unlikely to get an accurate and meaningful view of behaviour unless some information about these situations is available. Secondly, any suggestions for making helpful changes aren't going to be realistic and feasible unless the context is taken into account. Thirdly, it's much more natural and comfortable for the child to be seen in their usual situations.

When a psychologist does an observation, they may use a list of key points to be observed, they may time aspects of the observations very precisely, and they could use a published observation schedule, of which there are many. It's likely that they will make notes according to different features of the child's cognitive, emotional, social and physical development that are apparent during the session. Other important headings may include speech and language and independence skills. All or some of these areas may be the particular focus. Many newly qualified psychologists or psychologists in training wish for a comprehensive checklist that will cover everything possible; but in reality, as each observation is different, has a different purpose and involves unique children and situations, such a checklist doesn't exist. It takes many years of professional practice and ongoing professional development to carry out observations thoroughly, systematically and in a relevant way.

Think back to one of the big ideas from social psychology (Chapter 20): that behaviour results from the interplay between the person and all their characteristics and their context, i.e. **B = f (P x S)**. This next practical exercise is designed to make clear the key importance of different contexts in shaping the individual's behaviour.

Take a few minutes to observe your child in the following situations: at home watching television, playing with toys or at a family mealtime, in the park and at the shops. Make some brief notes under the following headings:

- Situation: place and activity (notes any others involved)
- Social behaviour: how they behave to others
- Emotions: range of emotions shown
- Physical behaviour: movement, co-ordination, hand skills
- Language.

When you read through your notes you may see some similar entries for different situations, but you're likely to also see some very different ones. When a psychologist undertakes an observation in this way, they pay close attention to the similarities and differences and start to formulate ideas, or hypotheses, about what is making a difference to the child's behaviour and observed abilities. They can then base their suggestions and recommendations on these ideas.

Psychometric tests and standardized tests in general are an important aspect of a psychologist's possible assessment practice, but their use can be contentious. These tests are produced and tried out with large numbers of people who are selected on the basis of being representative of the general population as a whole. The scores are analysed and the average scores calculated. These averages are known as the test norms, and norms are calculated usually in relation to specific age ranges. The tests must be carried out in a very consistent and standard way, hence the term 'standardized', and the aim is to achieve as objective a measure as possible. The tests are contentious for a number of reasons, including the following:

1. It's not usual for a great variation of scores, i.e. a range of scores between individuals and within individual scores, to exist. The test can't truly represent and reflect the complexity of individuals.
2. The test results do not, in themselves, lead to suggestions for what can be done in practical terms to help a child in the real-life situation of home or school. In other words, the applicability of the information gained from using the tests can be questionable.
3. A major criticism of standardized tests is that the tests can be culturally biased. For example, if the sample from which the test norms were gained includes only children born in the UK who speak English as their first language, and the test is undertaken with a child who speaks English as a second language, it will hardly be fair as it won't take into account differences in children's language backgrounds.
4. Tests of intelligence, known as psychometric, cognitive and IQ tests, are designed to assess an individual's ability to learn, but the term 'intelligence' is a problematic one (see below).

Much has been written about the concept of intelligence, and many have challenged traditional and accepted criteria, usually relating to academic excellence. Broadly speaking, intelligence is the ability of an individual to problem-solve and to use knowledge in particular and unique situations. For the traditional intelligence test, the capacity to do this is confined to academic situations and academic issues. Howard Gardner, an American academic psychologist, has produced a theory of **multiple intelligences** in which he includes not just academic intelligence but also intelligences to do with creativity, including music and art, and inter-personal and emotional ability. Another key name, particularly in relation to the idea of **emotional intelligence**, is Daniel Goleman. Emotional intelligence is the general term given to an individual's capacity to be aware of, to communicate and to constructively use their emotions; along with being sensitive to, and aware of, the emotions of others, and being skilful in relation to this.

Traditional intelligence tests aim to assess only the traditional intelligences. Think of the three most 'intelligent' people you know. Your choice will depend on your own definition of 'intelligence'. If you think about why you chose the individuals you did, you'll see that there can be many types of intelligence.

Some psychologists will not use psychometric assessment tests, but many do, arguing that these are a helpful part of their assessment 'tool-kit', as long as they are administered selectively and carefully and as part of an overall assessment that uses other methods and approaches. In this way, a broad range of information can be collected, analysed, interpreted and used on the basis of the psychologist's clinical experience, knowledge and judgement.

The key ideas

- Any involvement with a qualified (chartered) psychologist who works with individual children and young people starts with an assessment.
- Every assessment starts with a question or questions.
- In the UK, chartered psychologists must work within the ethical and professional practice guidelines of the British Psychological Society and are regulated by the Health Professions Council. Other countries have their own regulatory systems and associated guidelines, and some information about this is available in the References.
- Many methods of assessment exist, including interviews, observation, published tests and standardized tests, including psychometric tests.
- A number of problems are associated with psychometric assessments: they don't reflect individual complexity, the results lack practical application, there could be cultural bias, and they raise problems with definitions of intelligence.

23. Therapeutic work

... Pluck from the memory a rooted sorrow,
Raze out the written troubles of the brain
And with some sweet oblivious antidote
Cleanse the stuff'd bosom of that perilous stuff
Which weighs upon the heart ...

William Shakespeare, *Macbeth*

Humans are sentient or emotional beings. As such our emotional lives are hugely important and complicated, and can be difficult to understand. There's no recipe book or instruction manual for solving problems of an emotional nature, and we all have our own journeys and processes to work on throughout life, as children and as adults. For parents, this can be a somewhat daunting realization, as the well-being and progress of their children rests on them, as parents, being emotionally balanced and relatively settled. Sometimes skilled therapeutic help is needed. Problems can arise with the emotional development of children, and parents should feel able to access help as and when they need to do so.

THINK ABOUT IT

Look at this list of very common problems that children and young people can experience, and think about which ones might benefit from therapeutic support.

- Poor school work
- Bereavement
- Few social relationships
- Truancy
- Sibling rivalry
- Self-harm
- Bullying
- Dieting excessively
- Over-eating
- Tiredness
- Morbid thoughts about death, disease and disaster
- Alcohol abuse.

The question might just as easily have been, would any of these issues *not* benefit from therapy of some kind?

The acid test of whether or not an emotional problem warrants professional support is: to what degree is the issue interfering with, adversely affecting, or even blocking the child or young person's day-to-day life? There's some truth in the idea that the passage of time can reduce some difficulties, because children and young people are constantly developing, growing and adapting. In Chapter 12 on Lifespan Theory, Eric Erikson is quoted as saying that children aren't like Humpty Dumpty – they have the capacity to pull themselves together again. Certainly, a key belief among professionals using therapeutic approaches is that therapy can help this rebuilding of the self.

The way in which a therapist works with children and young people, and adults, is guided by the same principles as those described in the previous chapter on assessment. Many chartered psychologists do undertake work of a therapeutic nature but don't generally describe themselves as 'therapists'. Other professionals who aren't chartered psychologists, however, do have this title and work in accordance with the professional guidance of their own accreditation bodies. There are a number of specialist therapy organizations such as those devoted entirely to Cognitive Behavioural Therapy, Brief Solution-Focused Therapy and Family Therapy (all described below), which have their own training systems and professional bodies. An internet search will lead to whichever type you're interested in.

The largest and best-known organization for therapists in the UK is the British Association for Counselling and Psychotherapy (BACP). The BACP website states that its purpose is to 'enable access to ethical and effective psychological therapy by setting and monitoring of standards' (BACP website: http://www.bacp.co.uk/). The list of possible therapeutic approaches is long. The BACP website lists a large number of these, along with lists of approved practitioners and training bodies. Some equivalent bodies in other countries are listed in the References.

Below are some brief descriptions of a few therapeutic approaches that are especially relevant for work with children and young people, either individually or as part of family-based work, or possibly in other groups, for example in a school setting.

Cognitive Behavioural Therapy

Cognitive Behavioural Therapy (CBT) is probably one of the best-known approaches and is said to have the strongest evidence in terms of effectiveness. Aaron T. Beck wrote a book about 'cognitive therapy' in 1976, which was a time when behaviourist theory (see Chapter 4) was very much the popular approach to helping people with mental health issues. The basic idea in cognitive therapy was to work with and change the **thinking** and **learning** of individuals for the benefit of their overall psychological health and well-being. For example, people who are suffering from depression have a tendency to focus on their most sad and negative mood states. If they can be helped to think differently and locate happier thoughts and feelings more often, this can gradually improve their emotional state through seeing things differently and feeling in control more of the time.

Cognitive Behavioural Therapy, as the name suggests, uses a blend of cognitive and behavioural ideas and strategies. Most people experience days when they wake up feeling rather down, and if a number of things then happen to lower their mood further, they can get stuck in a way of thinking that makes them feel worse: 'This is just my luck – I always have problems'; 'I'm just a miserable and negative person'; 'Nothing good ever happens to me.' In CBT terminology this thinking style is described as featuring **negative automatic thoughts** or **thinking errors**. Thinking errors often involve over-generalizing thoughts, coming to conclusions after just one difficult happening or situation, exaggerating, all-or-nothing thinking, and people using lots of 'shoulds', 'musts' and 'oughts' in their internal and critical conversations with themselves.

If a cognitive behavioural therapist is involved, it's their task to challenge these thoughts. They help the person to increase their awareness of these thoughts and then assess how accurate and true they are. There are many ways to do this, but one of the most commonly used techniques is to get the person to keep a diary of their mood states each day, hour by hour, and rate the moods from 1 to 10, the best mood being 1 and the worst being 10. Invariably a range of mood ratings is produced, and the person can then be supported in looking at the best ratings, working out what they were doing/thinking at that time, where they were, who else was involved, how they behaved and so on. This is then very useful material for building the basis for feeling better more of the time.

You can try this out on yourself by using a diary sheet like the one on page 187, probably for at least a week, and then seeing which times and situations were the happiest.

When you've done this, even for just a week, you're likely to start seeing patterns. For example, there may be some activities and/or situations that are consistently linked with your best moods. This immediately highlights your capacity to be a happier/luckier/more even individual. It also shows you what you might do, or do more of, in order to feel that way more often, and to gain perspective during the times when you feel down.

The big idea behind CBT is that in helping a person to experience more psychological well-being, a number of aspects have to be taken into account. Originally these aspects were the individual's thoughts, feelings and behaviour. Since Beck's early work in the 1970s, two more elements – biological and environmental – have been added. All of these aspects affect each other and if one changes, then so will the others to some degree. The fact that people can be born with similar biological and/or environmental challenges certainly affects their progress through life, but to different degrees depending on the individual. CBT works on the principle that it's possible to effect some degree of positive change for anyone. Look at the diagram on page 188 to see how this works.

	MON	TUE	WED	THU	FRI	SAT	SUN
	Mood Behaviour Thoughts	Mood Behaviour Thoughts	Mood Behaviour Thoughts	Mood Behaviour Thoughts	Mood Behaviour Thoughts	Mood Behaviour Thoughts	Mood Behaviour Thoughts
Waking until 10							
10 until 12							
12 until 3							
3 until 6							
6 until 9							
9 until bedtime							

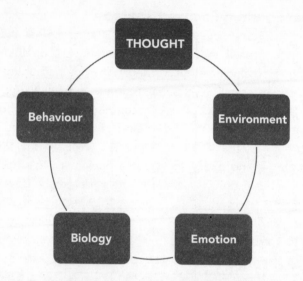

Factors influencing a person's psychological well-being: a CBT model

The use of CBT approaches with children and young people has begun to gather some momentum. Educational and clinical psychology training courses now feature training in the use of CBT. We have already looked at the idea that even very young children can be helped to learn new ways of thinking about themselves and their behaviour and learning, e.g. Bruner and Vygotsky's work (Chapters 6 and 7), and the effects of environment and relationships, e.g. Bronfenbrenner and Winnicott (Chapters 21 and 11). As for most aspects of modern-day child psychology, many theories contribute and build on each other in CBT.

Brief Solution-Focused Therapy

Brief Solution-Focused Therapy (BSFT) is another thera-peutic approach that has developed from a number of therapies, including Brief Strategic Therapy and Solution-Focused Therapy. Psychoanalytical and humanist psycho-logical theories have obviously contributed at some point as well. Firstly, the Brief Strategic Therapy aspect is to do with the fact that BSFT concentrates on using the skills, knowledge and experience that a person already has at their disposal, and it also aims to help the person develop better ways of living and working through setting and work-ing towards goals. This way of working is usually carried out in a small number of sessions or even a single session, unlike traditional psychoanalytical work, which takes much longer and could consist of up to several sessions a week over months or even years. Secondly, the Solution-Focused angle involves the individual doing just that, i.e. looking at and examining what is working and doing it more and better.

 Imagine in the previous exercise you found that you were particularly happy when you spent time walking. The BSFT therapist would ask you to carefully consider what made it possible for you to walk. You might say, having time and a reason to walk, being with others and/or being on your own. Perhaps having good all-weather clothing and footwear helped, and/or going to a favourite place and/or listening to an audiobook or music on headphones. The particular conditions and resources will vary from person to person, but it's possible, if you're clear what they are for you, that you can improve and/or find more of these and develop better strategies for everyday life.

Thinking about you as a parent, how is it possible to combine time with your child/children in a way that increases your own well-being? If you can do this, it's highly likely to have a good effect on the children's mood state too.

Another important idea from BSFT is that of developing a **future focus**. This is an essential part of the process because unless you believe that things could be different, and that with time and effort you can help them to be different, you stay firmly locked into the present – or perhaps worse still, the past.

 Consider the situation that many parents of teenagers find themselves in. Lots of teenagers seem to want to choose quite chaotic lives, which is apparent from the state of their bedrooms. The parent who has no hope of anything being different, in the worst-case scenario, would either slavishly clear up the mess and run around most of the time after their son or daughter, or let the mess build up to levels that threatened general health and safety.

In fact a lot of psychological and physical energy goes into this quite typical problem. Parents who have a **future focus** use ideas like building rewards into more clean and tidy behaviour, involving the young person in decorating their own room and choosing furniture and fittings, and ensuring that the teenager has some private and uninterrupted space for themselves. There are many creative solutions to this problem, but they are possible only if some hope for the future exists.

Family Therapy

Many professionals such as social workers, education welfare officers, youth offender workers and teachers recognize the importance of working with the child within their family system. Instead of focusing on the child separately, they can then use their knowledge of the family and everyday family life to put into place interventions and support that use the family's strengths and resources and address the problem areas. Family therapy, like the other therapies mentioned in this chapter, is a highly specialist area and some key figures have contributed to its development and the different ways of working, such as Salvador Minuchin, John Bowlby (see Chapter 11) and Gill Gorrell-Barnes.

Some fascinating theory has developed about the ways in which family members can interact, the rules, spoken and unspoken, that govern these interactions, and the underlying beliefs and attributions. A seemingly simple example might be to reflect on a routine part of your own family life.

Think about your usual evening meal. Think about how the meal is planned, made, eaten and cleared up. Then think about who is involved, their roles and responsibilities, and where the meal takes place. Imagine you were writing the rules for all of this.

On page 193 is a chart for you to complete. The first item is completed as an example.

Common areas that a family therapist might explore are communication, power dynamics, patterns of closeness, disconnectedness, traditions in the family and within the extended family, conflict, loss and separation. The work of any therapist is complicated and requires high levels of skill, training and support from colleagues, but perhaps that of a family therapist is even more so, as there's so much to take into account.

Generally speaking, family therapy will take place over a number of months, or longer in some cases. It's possible for a single therapist or even a team of therapists to be involved, and the initial sessions will be devoted to 'mapping out' the family composition. The usual way is to use a **genogram**, a basic example of which is shown on page 194. This is a genogram of a single-parent family in which

	WHO	HOW	WHERE	RULE/S *Spoken Unspoken*
PLANNING	Dad Mum	Makes lists, shops Organizes kitchen, finds out who is eating	At home and online	*Dad is a good organizer and money-manager* Dad is in charge
PREPARATION				
EATING				
CLEARING UP				

the parents were divorced and the father had died, with two children, a younger boy and an older girl. The older sibling is usually placed on the left.

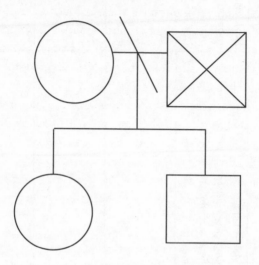

An example of a genogram

You could make a genogram of your own immediate family. Females are shown as circles and males as squares. Parents go at the top and children below. If the parents are divorced or not together, then a diagonal line is used between them; and if someone has died, this is shown by a cross.

Art Therapy

This is an ideal way of working with children, as it's an activity that most enjoy, a variety of materials can be used, and they are likely to experience the approach as a play activity. The drawings, paintings and collages or models that emerge from sessions with an art therapist are often so vivid as almost to speak for themselves. The type of artwork produced will be influenced by how the therapist explains and introduces the session. Sometimes the therapy can be very free-flowing and the children will produce whatever they feel like doing at any point. Other times the therapist may introduce a theme, ask a question or give explicit instructions. It really depends on how 'interpretative' the art therapist is, and how much she/he can help the child to explain their creations.

 If your child is of nursery or infant age, try giving them a piece of plain paper and one coloured drawing crayon. Draw a squiggly line on the paper and ask the child to turn it into something. Then give them the choice of several different pieces of coloured paper and a whole pot of coloured crayons. Compare the results of these two exercises. At the very least it will give you an idea of your child's imagination, wish to experiment or follow instructions, enjoyment in using colour, drawing skills, confidence and concentration, plus many other aspects of their approach to art activities.

Some art-based assessment instruments and methods for gauging a child's stage of emotional development are available, and these generally use the child's drawing of a person, the family, or common objects such as a mouse or a cat, to judge their stage of emotional development. Such assessment draws heavily on the psychologist's level of clinical experience and skill in making sure that the child is at ease and able to produce their best and most representative work. It also draws on the clinician's knowledge of various theories of child development such as psychoanalytical theory, attachment theory, and systems theories such as Bronfenbrenner's work.

Play Therapy

Imaginative play can be viewed as a major resource by which children can cope immediately with the cognitive, affective and social demands of growing up.

Jerome Singer

The importance of children's play is key to this approach, as is the idea that children have an innate tendency to make sense of and work through difficulties of a psychological nature. As with other therapeutic ways of working, the links with a range of psychological theories, and particularly those relating to child development, are strong. Neuropsychological research is gradually making links between the effects of trauma, including bereavement, on neurological development, health and behaviour, and play therapy is viewed as one way of addressing the effects of traumatic experience on children.

 Spend a little time, no more than ten minutes, observing your child at play. What are they doing that could have benefits for:

- Physical development – either large or gross movements such as running, climbing, jumping, or small or fine movements such as picking up small objects, using objects like bricks, crayons.
- Emotional or affective development – which emotions do they show and express in their words, body movements and actions?
- Social development – speech and/or behaviour that affects or is affected by others, real and imaginary.
- Cognitive development – language, problem-solving, learning in general.

If you note down your observations, the list is likely to be a long one. You can think about these and use your reflections to consider how to make your child's play even richer – but one word of caution: over-structuring or organizing a child's play is not recommended. They will have many years of structured play and learning in their educational experience, and it's important that play is as natural and spontaneous as possible for the child at home.

Play therapy developed originally in the US and Canada, but over the last two to three decades it has been practised increasingly in the UK, and a number of training courses now exist here. The British Association of Play Therapists emphasizes the importance of the therapist and child relationship, the provision of a safe space and a range of appropriate play materials, and facilities for supporting healing. (Details of organizations from other countries are listed in the References.) As with art therapy, there are many approaches used by play therapists, ranging from quite directive methods with particular ways of working, structuring sessions and activities, to much more free-flowing sessions in which the child exercises high levels of choice. Some therapists use story-telling and puppet work.

As with other therapeutic methods, it's important that continuity and safety are ensured within and between sessions, and the child's usual living situation and context should be taken into account when deciding whether or not they would benefit from play therapy. For example, a child who is 'in care' and for whom long-term care arrangements are not established, may not be able to build on the therapeutic work they do in sessions.

This highlights the importance of making strong links and working with the child's carer/s, as for all interventions with children and young people.

REMEMBER THIS!!!

Key points about therapeutic work using child psychology

- Problems can arise with the emotional development of children, and if these obstruct their usual everyday life, behaviour and/or learning, then it may be appropriate to organize professional therapeutic help.

- A wide range of therapeutic approaches and associated organizations exist, including CBT, BSFT, Family Therapy, Art Therapy and Play Therapy, which are all commonly used with children, young people and families.

- Major professional bodies exist to ensure safe, ethical and effective professional therapy practice.

- The effectiveness of professional therapy arises from strong links with appropriate theory.

- Work with children and young people should involve work with their primary carers and be undertaken in a way that is compatible with their family and living situation.

FINAL POINTS

24. Parenting and caring

Many words of wisdom have been written about the phe-
nomenon that is a family – and a great deal that lack wisdom
also. Virginia Axline, an American humanistic psychologist
who contributed to the creation of play therapy, in my view
has some very wise things to say. She writes of the complex and difficult task of having and raising children and
suggests that the parenting couple can be compared to
two powerful and complicated business dynasties coming
together to produce a new and completely unique product – a baby – which they care about passionately. This is
a useful analogy because it highlights not only the history
of each couple, their present challenges and their future
hopes and aims, but it also hints at the extended family
and culture from which each parent comes. In addition, the
parents, especially first-time parents, have to engage in a
job for which they have had no formal training, and about
which everyone else seems to hold a view and to consider
their viewpoint the best.

The British Psychological Society produced a report
in 2007 about how educational psychologists could work
best with parents and carers. In this report they describe

the educational psychologist's contribution to working with the parent/carer in partnership for the best interests of the child, sometimes as an advocate or voice for the parent, and also in parent-training work. Underpinning the whole report is the principle and recognition that parents/carers have an in-depth knowledge of the child, the child's background, their living, learning and cultural situations, and can also support the child's voice.

It wouldn't make sense in a book on child psychology not to acknowledge the fundamental importance of parenting and caring to children's learning, behaviour and emotional development. This is implicit to every theory and approach described. In this chapter I will summarize some of what psychologists who work particularly with children and young people have found out about effective parenting and caring. I will do this through brief fictional examples of childhood challenges that have been supported with child psychology. Each case refers to *some* of the theories that have been described in this book.

Bethany

Twelve-year-old Bethany was born with congenital heart disease. As a result, her parents were very protective of her, had numerous checkups and hospital stays to organize, and had to ensure that she kept up with schoolwork that was missed as a result. Obviously, there were many aspects of the family's life that were affected, and lots of things that couldn't be planned for in the usual way. Bethany was making good progress in most areas but she and her younger brother Tom were having many arguments, which spoilt family life in general. The parents decided to get some advice and support from the clinical psychologist employed by the hospital that Bethany attended. Her work started with an assessment drawing on **Ecological Systems Theory** of the family situation, through talking to the parents and children and also a grandmother who cared for Tom during Bethany's hospital visits. She then set up a programme using some **Behaviourist** and **Motivation Theory** ideas in which Tom and Bethany were rewarded in different ways, i.e. actual physical rewards, social rewards and self-rewards, for getting on well. She also used ideas from **Family Therapy** in her meetings with the family. The situation improved and was greatly helped by the *warmth* of the parents' approach, which research on parenting shows is key.

Joseph

Joseph was diagnosed as being clinically obese on his seventh birthday. He was a happy boy on the whole, but the quality of his life was reduced because of teasing from other pupils. This reached a point at which Joseph started to feign stomach ache in order to miss school, and his attendance dropped so far that an education welfare officer had to visit his home, subsequently asking the school's educational psychologist (EP) to work with Joseph and his family. Although it seemed obvious that Joseph's problems were all about his size, the underlying reasons for his over-eating and lack of physical activity hadn't been explored systematically up until now, so the EP spoke with school staff including lunchtime supervisors and teachers, family members, Joseph's doctor and Joseph himself, and she also did some observations of Joseph at home and at school, and some individual work with him. She drew on **Personal Construct Theory** and found out what Joseph's constructs (ideas and beliefs) about eating and exercise were all about. She also did some **cognitive** assessment to make sure that he didn't have any obvious learning difficulties. She discovered that Joseph and his mother had some complicated beliefs about eating, relating to infancy when there were problems with being weaned (**Psychodynamic Theory**). When this was clarified, it was then possible to set up some support for mother and Joseph through counselling, and also a programme on healthy living at school, designed for the entire class. Two of the things that really helped were Joseph's mother's very positive attitude and enthusiasm about his school, which she talked about with Joseph. *Parental positivity about education* and *enthusiasm* are qualities that research has shown to be very important to children's progress.

Sharon

Sharon was only five when her mother lost a baby. In many ways she didn't understand why her mum was so sad, and she couldn't make sense of the bereavement and loss involved. However, her play behaviour caused a lot of concern at school. She spent a lot of time in the home corner and in the playground, making up games about dead babies and talking about people, especially mummies, dying, and about being told off for this. The teacher had no idea what had happened until she asked Sharon's mum to come in for a meeting. The teacher used **humanistic** psychology principles in her work and gave Sharon's mother a chance to talk openly about the tragedy. She also consulted with the school's EP, who advised on other sources of support for the family and who, using her knowledge of **Lifespan Theory**, was able to suggest ways in which Sharon could be expected to understand and be supported. Gradually, with various forms of support and the intelligent and consistent parenting that was available, Sharon gained perspective and her play resumed more usual forms. *Intelligence and consistency* are qualities that research has identified in ideal parenting.

Bradley

Bradley was eight years old and struggling with reading and writing. He had been identified as having learning difficulties, and his teacher and the school's special educational needs co-ordinator (SENCo) gave him extra learning support and placed him on the school's register of special needs. Many different teaching and learning arrangements were put in place for him, and his progress carefully monitored and reviewed in regular meetings with his carers. Because he wasn't making progress, the school decided to prioritize him for some input from their educational psychologist. The psychologist consulted with home and school, observed Bradley in class, looked through his schoolwork and the school records and did some individual assessment work with him, including some dynamic assessment, drawing on **Vygotskian Theory**, **Information-Processing Theories** and **Neuropsychology Theory**. Bradley was found to have specific learning difficulties of a dyslexic nature, and his Individual Education Plan was rewritten to include some specialist dyslexia learning support and use of word-processing and computer programs. He steadily made more progress and was encouraged by his carers and school staff to view this as being due to his own efforts, in line with **Motivation Theory**, and to the special arrangements that had been put into place. His carers *communicated well and had high aspirations* for Bradley, which are well-defined characteristics of effective parenting.

Key points about findings from research on parenting

The most important qualities and attitudes associated with effective parenting include:

- High aspirations
- Positive talk about education
- Intelligence
- Warmth
- Communicative ability
- Enthusiasm
- Stability/continuity.

25. Summary

*All happy families are alike; each unhappy family
is unhappy in its own way.*

Leo Tolstoy

Tolstoy's words ring equally true when 'child' or 'young person' is substituted for 'family'. Writing this book and doing justice to the huge and complex subject of child psychology was an exciting challenge, but no more so than starting a new piece of work with a child, young person or family.

It's best to think of this book as a stepping stone or a starting point that you may (or may not) wish to explore further. I don't claim to have exhausted the range of possible theories and theorists but, as I said, it's a start. One theory that hasn't been mentioned here, but with which it seems appropriate to finish, is **Gestalt Theory**. In this theory, learning, reproduction, striving, emotional attitude, thinking and behaviour must be viewed in their entirety, taking into account everything that the person and the context brings in interaction with every other part. Also, the idea that the whole is different – better or worse – to the sum of the parts is important. This is why it's important to look at and apply as wide and full an account of child development as possible. The final quotation is from Fritz Perls, who developed Gestalt Theory and therapy, neither of which are in vogue at this time but both of which have certainly contributed to many other theories and ways of working:

> *I do my thing, and you do your thing*
> *I am not in this world to live up to your expectations*
> *And you are not in this world to live up to mine*
> *You are you, and I am I,*
> *And if by chance we find each other, it's beautiful,*
> *If not, it can't be helped.*

Fritz Perls

You will have your own views on this, but speaking personally, I don't entirely agree – and probably because of this I became a psychologist. This book is written because of my belief that positive psychology can offer a lot to the process of finding each other, and nowhere more so than in the work involved in being a parent. I have found this is the case from both my experience as an educational psychologist and as a parent of four children. I very much hope that the 'Gestalt' of this book will contribute to your experience.

REFERENCES

American Psychological Association: www.apa.org/

American Art Therapy Organization: www.arttherapy.org/

Australian Psychological Society: www.psychology.org.au/

British Association for Behavioural and Cognitive
Psychotherapy: www.babcp.com/

British Association for Counselling and Psychotherapy:
www.bacp.co.uk/

British Association of Art Therapy: www.baat.org/

British Psychological Society: www.bps.org.uk/

Canadian Psychological Association: www.cpa.ca/

European Federation of Psychologists' Associations:
www.efpa.eu/

International Association for Analytical Psychology:
www.iaap.org/

International Society for Child and Play Therapy:
www.playtherapy.org/

Mind: www.mind.org.uk/

National Children's Bureau: www.ncb.org.uk/

New Zealand Psychological Society:
www.psychology.org.nz/

Psychological Society of South Africa: www.psyssa.com/

Index